CLOSET CULTIVATOR

CLOSET CULTIVATOR

ED ROSENTHAL

QUICK AMERICAN ARCHIVES

Published by Quick American Archives
Oakland, California

Copyright © 1999 Ed Rosenthal

Photos: Aphid, Mite, Thrip, Whitefly © Ohio State University
Photo: Indoor garden using styrofoam™ containers © Tom Flowers
Project Manager: S. Rose
Editing: J. Abrahms and D. Zippel
Line Editing: M. Valletta
Photo Research: M. White
Color Section: Pepper Design
Illustration: J. E. McCreary

Printed in the U.S.A. by Publishers Express Press

Dedicated to Ron Turner and Last Gasp for providing a platform for the unconventional, the questionable, and the controversial.

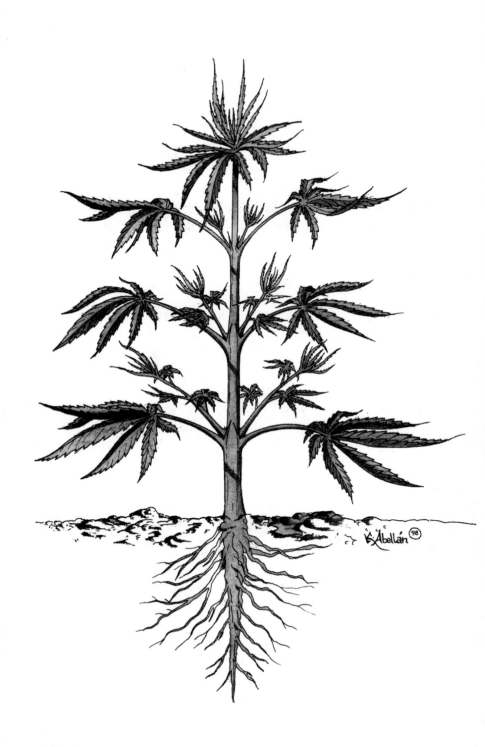

CONTENTS

INTRODUCTION

The purpose of this book is to show how marijuana is grown in a small space. This is not complicated, and requires little effort. The easy-to-follow instructions explain everything needed to set up and grow a small indoor garden that will produce large crops of high-quality buds.

Using this guide, a person would be able to grow enough bud to satisfy all of his or her needs. Embarking on this great new adventure means that the high prices and risks involved with obtaining marijuana will soon be in the past.

The plants' bounty is the primary motivation for most growers. There is nothing quite the same as homegrown, whether it's tomatoes or herb. Most home growers think that the fruit of their labor is the sweetest and most nourishing.

Most people who have grown marijuana say they have found the garden rewarding in many ways besides the crop's yield. This may be because marijuana plants are fast-growing and, like most annuals, they usually complete their life cycle in a few months. Germination, early growth, adolescence, sexual ripening, and senescence all occur within 90 days.

Another reason people enjoy growing is that the plants quickly respond to changes in their environment. We notice the way they grow, much as we notice the growth of babies or young pets. Unlike other annuals, marijuana has separate male and female plants; this allows us to personify them.

Finally, being in a garden, tending to the plants, and watching them grow is a soothing, even healing, experience. A well-located garden, just a door away, makes access to such a green haven very convenient. Even in deepest winter, this lush greenery is there to enjoy.

Although growing marijuana is illegal almost everywhere, one or more of these factors may drive a person to start a garden of their own. If that's the case, this book is the best way to begin.

CHAPTER 1

PLANNING

Nothing should be done prematurely. Before potential growers do anything else, buy anything else, or make any other effort toward gardening in any way, they should READ THIS BOOK! They should digest enough of the information here to make intelligent decisions as to how big a garden will be needed, where to place it, and what techniques they will want to use.

It goes without saying that growers should have a clear idea of their goals. This idea serves as a guide when the garden is designed. The plan for the garden should be written and drawn so that it can be consulted to keep on track. Having a careful plan also saves money, because growers won't wind up purchasing materials that they don't need. Once the garden has been set up, these descriptions are not needed and should be discarded for safety reasons.

All the information needed to set up a garden may not be absorbed on a first reading. Read the book again. Carrying out the project correctly the first time will save months on the learning curve.

CHAPTER 2

SETTING GOALS

The modern indoor marijuana garden is high-yielding because it optimizes growing conditions for the plants, helping them achieve their full potential. Indoors, marijuana is a very productive plant. Using the techniques described in this book, a gardener can grow quite a bit of bud in a small space. On the average, growers should expect to harvest about one-quarter to one ounce of bud from one square foot (ft²) of growing space in the finishing room.

Obviously, a very large space is not necessary to grow a productive garden. To put this in perspective, a garden set up in a space four feet by four feet (16 square feet), can produce between three and five crops a year, each yielding between one-quarter to one pound or more. This does not mean that the first crop, or every crop, will yield this much, but once the grower has some hands-on experience, this is what may be expected.

In addition to the flowering room we've just described, a smaller space may be needed for the vegetative growth stage. Mother plants and cuttings grow in this section, which keeps the main garden supplied. No additional space is required if there is an outside source for these plants. If not, a separate garden, on a different light regimen, is required. This garden requires about a one-half square foot area for each square foot in the flowering room.

Potential growers should figure out how much marijuana they actually use during the year. Then they should estimate the amount they would use if they had free access to good bud. For each ounce, figure that an average of about one-and-one-half square feet in the flowering space will be necessary, using the techniques described in this book. For instance, if one-quarter ounce per week would be used—an ounce per month—only three to four ounces would need to be grown for each harvest; this indicates that the grower would need a constantly growing garden of only six to eight square feet.

Smaller gardens are easier to maintain than larger ones. Problems that don't occur or are easy to solve in small gardens will often require much more elaborate solutions in larger ones. The modern indoor garden is high-yielding because it optimizes growing conditions for the plants, helping them achieve their full potential. This type of garden saves space, energy, and labor and produces the best results: a large yield of high-quality bud.

CHAPTER 3

WHAT DO MARIJUANA PLANTS WANT AND NEED?

Growing on its own, marijuana is a sun-loving plant that thrives in a nutrient-rich, well-drained soil.

Marijuana has several distinct stages in its life cycle. The first is germination from seed. Next, the plant usually goes through a rapid vegetative growth stage, in which it grows its infrastructure and expends its energy growing new branches and leaves. The last stages are the reproductive ones.

During reproductive growth, the plant puts its resources into flower production. Marijuana has separate male and female plants. The part of the plant that growers aim to produce is the bud, which consists of masses of unfertilized female flowers. If the flowers are fertilized with male pollen, the plant stops producing flowers and devotes its energy to the developing seed. For this reason, the male plants are removed from the garden as soon as they are detected.

All green growing plants require light, space for their foliage, space and a suitable growing medium for their roots, water, nutrients, the gases oxygen and carbon dioxide, and suitable temperatures. For a plant to grow well, all its needs must be met.

Indoors, growers create the environment for the plants, so they will be concerned with all these factors. We'll be discussing them throughout the book.

Getting the garden to its ideal state takes a bit of investment. Luckily, it doesn't have to be done all at once. A garden can be set up even with the bare essentials. A light with a timer and some planting containers sown with high-quality seeds will get a grower started. Improvements can be added incrementally.

CHAPTER 4

CHOOSING THE SPACE

Choosing the right space to grow the plants in may be the most important decision a grower makes. Everything else about the garden and the way the plants are grown will be influenced by the choice of space.

Almost any space can be converted to a growing area. However, some are easier to develop than others. To grow a conventional garden, the space must be at least five feet high. It should have access to electricity and there should be some means of ventilation. The perfect space would have a concrete or tile floor and floor drains, a built-in ventilator system, and an air intake source near the floor. Of course, very few spaces are like this.

Based on the goals worked out in Chapter 1, growers should decide how much space they need and where they will find it. Many home growers use an area of 16 square feet as the flowering section of their garden. Usable spaces may be found in the following locations:

EIGHT SQUARE FEET

2' × 4'—Some closets, an armoire, a covered shelf area

3' × 3'—A utility room

1' × 8'—Some closets, a space behind curtains in a room

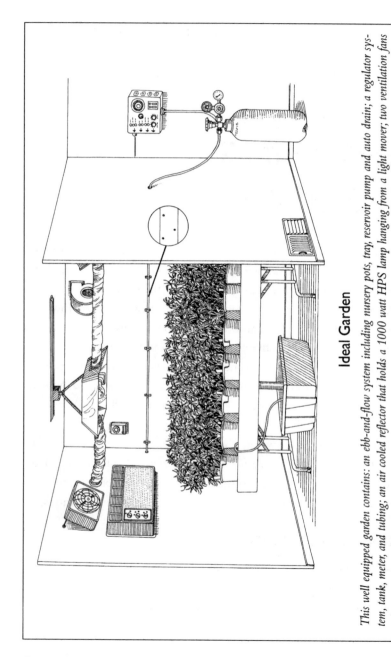

Ideal Garden

This well equipped garden contains: an ebb-and-flow system including nursery pots, tray, reservoir pump and auto drain; a regulator system, tank, meter, and tubing; an air cooled reflector that holds a 1000 watt HPS lamp hanging from a light mover; two ventilation fans on opposite sides of the garden; a humidistat/thermostat regulating a squirrel fan, vents and an air conditioner to the cool room.

SIXTEEN SQUARE FEET

2' × 8'—Some closets, the side of a room

3' × 5'—A corner or part of a room, or a space in a garage

4' × 4'—A closet or a space in a room

THIRTY-TWO SQUARE FEET

Two separate 16-square-foot gardens.

3' × 11'— One side of a room

4' × 8'— A part of a room or a space in a wider area,
          such as an attic or basement

Gardens should be designed so that the grower has easy access to the entire space. This is usually not too hard to do. The space should be no wider than five feet. Most gardeners find two-and-one-half to three feet a comfortable reach and working distance. Larger growing areas should be designed with aisles so that plants can be attended easily. Aisles with a width of one-and-one-half to two feet are easy to navigate and work in.

Occasionally, growers place the planting units on wheels so that they can be easily moved, eliminating the need for most aisles.

If needed, the vegetative section of the garden should be about one-half to one-third the area of the flowering section. It requires a total height of three feet. The plants from this section will eventually be transferred to the flowering section.

Even if growers don't start with an ideal space, a near-perfect environment for the plants can still be created. When the plants are in this environment, they grow very quickly and produce buds to their genetic potential.

Horizontal Positioning

Twisting plants to grow in a horizontal position helps them avoid excess light as they develop and allows them to be grown in a space with low ceilings.

Selective Pruning

Plants can be pruned to flatness to prevent branches from growing at 90 degree angles, maximizing growth in a limited space.

NOVEL GARDENS

Although the gardens described above are quite small, they are not small enough for some circumstances. Still, many people want to try their hand at growing marijuana. Luckily, cannabis has the ability to adapt to unusual growing conditions. Here are some novel ways in which it can be grown.

TRAINING TO A FENCE

Marijuana can be controlled to eliminate most of its three-dimensional shape by tying the branches to a fence. Imagine a space fifty inches wide against a wall, fifteen inches deep and six feet high. The walls are covered with aluminum foil. Plastic garden fencing, used to hold vine such as peas and tomatoes, is stretched over a frame of one-foot-by-two-feet and placed against the wall. The plants are kept tied to the fencing as they grow, and a bank of 8 four-foot fluorescent lights is placed on the floor, lighting the flat garden.

HORIZONTALIZING

Marijuana uses gravity to sense which direction is up, and then grows in that direction. When a plant that has been growing normally is placed on its side, new growth reorients itself and starts growing upward again. Short spaces can sometimes be maximized by placing plants horizontally.

SELECTIVE PRUNING

Marijuana grows branches in four directions: first in opposite pairs, and then alternating. If two opposite sides of the plant are pruned, it grows flat naturally.

PLANTS IN A SHORT SPACE

A space is only two-and-one-half feet high, thirteen inches wide, and five feet long. A four-tube fluorescent unit, designed for ceiling installation, is placed on the top. The plants grow in four-inch-deep, twelve-inch-wide trays, which are each two feet long. The plants are spaced two across every six inches for a total of eight per tray. They are forced to flower as soon as they are six inches tall, and are only fifteen inches tall at maturity.

CHAPTER 5

Growing Methods: Soil or Hydroponic Gardening

For the plant to thrive, its roots must have a healthy environment in which to live. Plants function best when they have plenty of nutrient-rich water, oxygen, and mild temperatures.

There are many ways to meet these conditions indoors. First, gardeners must choose whether they wish to grow the plants in pots with a planting mix or hydroponically. Each method has its advantages.

Most people have grown plants indoors in a potting mix. Planting marijuana can be as easy as filling containers with planting medium. The advantages of planting mixes are that they are inexpensive and easy to use. They grow good plants, and most people are familiar with them. However, since the amount of nutrients in the planting mix is limited, they are eventually used up by the plant and more will have to be supplied in solution with water.

Many marijuana growers use hydroponics, which is the process of growing marijuana in an inert medium. All nutrients are supplied in a water solution. When everything goes right in a hydroponic system, the growth rate and yield of the garden increases considerably, and in the long run, it is easier and more convenient than using planting mixes, especially for large gardens. However, hydroponic systems are more finicky than planting mediums.

Hydroponics is new to most people, but hydroponic techniques are actually easier to maintain than soil systems once the techniques are mastered. Water and nutrient problems are largely eliminated and the grower has more control of garden conditions.

Both methods work, and are effective means of growing marijuana. Some people contend that organic, soil-grown marijuana is tastier than hydro grass. I have never been able to tell the difference. Growers should go with what feels comfortable.

CHAPTER 6

GROWING IN PLANTING MIX

A grower should choose and plan for the size plant desired, whether it will be grown in planting mix or hydroponically. This raises questions of style and legal implications regarding the number of plants. Some people prefer to grow larger plants using a space of two to four square feet. (This is achieved spacing plants approximately every one-and-one-half and two feet, respectively.) Gardens with these plants take 20 to 35 days to get to the flowering stage. Smaller plants take less time to reach the flowering stage. Plants growing one per square foot take 15 to 20 days to reach the right size to force flowering. With plants growing four per square foot, the vegetative growth stage is ten days.

Once forced to flower, the plants ripen in 55 to 90 days, depending on the variety. When the plants are forced to flower while they are small, the time to harvest can be reduced up to 30 days because less time is spent in vegetative growth. This is a time savings of up to 33%.

There are several drawbacks to growing a larger number of smaller plants to get the same yield. First, it requires a little extra work, since more plants are involved. The legal situation also presents a problem when large numbers of plants are grown. When sentencing, many jurisdictions, as well as the federal government, rely on plant counts rather than weight in judging whether material was intended for sale. One large plant yielding more than several small plants is considered a less serious offense.

SIZE OF CONTAINERS

The following chart shows the size of the container, the number of cubic inches and the appropriate plant size for a circular tapered container.

It also shows the maximum height of the plant that each container easily supports. Plants can be potted up from smaller sizes to larger ones as they grow. This saves quite a bit of space in the garden. Plants

SIZE OF APPROPRIATE CONTAINER

CONTAINER SIZE	CUBIC INCHES OF MEDIUM	PLANT HEIGHT	USUAL AGE
2"	8	Seed/Clone-8"	Veg-20 Days
3"	15	Seed-Clone	Veg-30 Days
4"	40	Seed-Clone/16"	Veg-40 Days
5"	80	Seed- Flower at 6"	Veg through Flowering
6"	80	Flower at 8"	Veg-50 Days through Flowering
8"	315	Seed-35 Flower at 10–12"	Veg-40-60 Days
10"	550	Seed-50 Flower at 15"	Veg-70 Days through Flowering

growing in a "sea-of-green" system, close to each other and forced to flower when they are small, do not need containers larger than four or six inches.

Planting containers should have good drainage: several holes at the bottom of the container to allow water to drain out. This is extremely important, because soggy medium is not good for the roots and will hurt or kill the plant.

Seeds or clones can be started in small containers and then transplanted to larger ones as the plants grow. Planting and transplanting are covered in Chapter 16, "Care During Vegetative Growth."

THE PLANTING MIX

Marijuana adapts easily to container growing and many different kinds of planting mixes can be used to grow it. Most marijuana growers buy prepared potting mixes. These mixes are usually not really soil at all, but are peat moss or bark-based mediums. These have been engineered for texture, water, and nutrient-holding capacity. Unless a medium has been enriched, it has little nutrient matter of its own. Fertilizers must be added at planting time or during watering.

If the grower regularly buys a general planting mix for houseplants that is satisfactory, it can be used for this new garden. If the grower is unfamiliar with specific brands, he or she should look for one that says "pH-balanced," which should be in the mid-6 range. It should be recommended for most houseplants and for starting seeds. If the potting mix ingredient list states that it contains humus, compost, or soil, it should also state that the mix is pasteurized or sterilized.

Many potting mixes have been supplemented with a small amount of nutrients, using organic sources, fertilizers, or both. Most mixes, even when they list their supplemental ingredients, need additional fertilization supplied through water-soluble fertilizers. For most growers, planting mixes are the way to go.

Some gardeners prefer to make their own mix. I used to recommend this highly, but over the years the quality of planting mixes has increased, so this is not as imperative as it was years ago. Still, when growers make their own mixes, they can tailor them to their needs. Another possibility is to "customize" a prepared mix.

The most important consideration is to create a medium that drains well, yet has good moisture-holding capacity. Some of the ingredients are organic in nature; that is, they are composed of carbon-based products created by living organisms. They will absorb the fertilizers as microorganisms living in the mix use the planting mix and nutrients as food. This is why these materials act as buffers: they absorb excess nutrients and release them gradually.

MIX INGREDIENTS
ORGANIC INGREDIENTS

Bark absorbs some water and promotes drainage. It comes chipped to various sizes and is sterile. It can be used in place of lava or hydrostone, and can also be used as a medium by itself. Its disadvantages are that it deteriorates to compost as the bacteria feed on the nutrient-rich water and used alone, it holds relatively little moisture so it must be irrigated often. For small pots, use 1/4" to 1/2" pieces. In larger pots, you can use bigger pieces to maintain adequate drainage. Many commercial planting mixes use finely chopped or ground bark as the main ingredient.

Compost is composed of plant matter processed by microorganisms. It is not necessarily rich in nutrients, but is teeming with life that is beneficial to plant roots. It should smell earthy. It can be taken from a pile that has been "steamed"—that is, treated with vented vapor as the temperature rises to about 160°F, killing pathogens. Compost is also available at nurseries. Prebagged compost is usually pasteurized or sterilized, but there is a quality range: some companies sell chopped plant by-products as compost, while others sell thoroughly processed material. Before buying, a grower should examine the compost and read the ingredients on the label.

Humus is plant material that has decomposed anaerobically, in water. It is spongy and very fine, and holds water well. It contains many plant hormones and growth regulators naturally produced by the decomposing organisms. As a planting mix ingredient, it promotes microbial life and nutrient absorption.

Peat moss is decomposed moss that is mined from Canadian peat bogs. It holds enormous amounts of water and is used in many commercial planting mixes because of its nutrient-buffering ability. Use only "pH-adjusted" or "pH-balanced" peat. Peat is fine and crumbly, and resists wetting, so it should be premoistened in the bag using water with an added wetting agent or detergent (one teaspoon per gallon).

Topsoil is a natural mix of minerals and organics that is rich in nutrients and fair in its water-holding properties. It makes an excellent ingredient for a planting mix, but should not be used alone because of drainage and texture problems. Only pasteurized or sterilized soil should be used.

Worm castings are plant matter digested and concentrated by worms into a nutrient-rich, biologically active, earthy-smelling substance called vermipost. It has a fine texture and holds water moderately well. When it dries, it clumps into hard, brittle pieces, so it should be thoroughly mixed with the other ingredients.

MINERAL INGREDIENTS

The following are mineral ingredients. All are virtually inert. They have no nutrients and don't interact with the water-nutrient solution.

Gravel is composed of small stones. It promotes drainage and holds water on its surface. Small-sized pebbles or aquarium gravel is usually used in mixes. It can be used at the bottoms of containers to give them additional weight.

Perlite is an extremely lightweight puffed volcanic glass. It has a pitted surface, which holds water particles. It is hard to the touch and does not break down. It comes in several grades. The fine grade can be used for germination or cuttings, but only the coarse or medium size should be used in potting mixes. Dry perlite is very dusty. The bag should be watered before the material is removed, and a respirator mask should also be used, to avoid inhalation of the dust.

Sand promotes drainage and keeps the mix from caking. Both horticultural and construction sand can be used, but avoid limestone sand if possible. Sand is very heavy and has largely been replaced by perlite and vermiculite. Sand can be used to add weight to the containers if there is a chance that they may tip over.

Vermiculite is composed of mica that has been "popped" using heat. It is very lightweight and absorbs many times its weight in water, but it also promotes good drainage. It comes in various grades. For seed starting, cuttings, and plants in small containers, the fine size is used. For most containers, use either the medium or large-size pieces. Dry vermiculite is dusty and should be watered before it is removed from the container. A respirator mask should be used, too, since vermiculite contains small amounts of asbestos.

POTTING MIXES

There is no one perfect mix. All of the mixes that are described here will work well. The choice of a mix depends on personal preference. There are too many possibilities to describe here, but here are some typical ones.

ORGANIC MIXES

The following planting mixes are designed to be used as "soil" in containers if growers want to mix their own. They contain some organic ingredients, which supply some nutrients and buffer the fertilizers supplied when watering. All measurements are by volume.

1. One part each: perlite, vermiculite, worm castings, and humus. Lightweight; good drainage, so it is hard to overwater. It contains high amounts of nutrients and is filled with microbial life. This mix promotes vegetative growth.

2. One part each: perlite; vermiculite; peat moss, compost or humus; and worm castings. Good drainage, high in microbial life, not as rich in nutrients as #1.

3. One part each: compost or humus; aquarium gravel; peat moss; perlite; vermiculite; worm castings. A heavier medium that drains well.

4. Two parts each: vermiculite and perlite; one part compost, humus, or worm castings. Good drainage, little nutrient matter, but filled with beneficial organisms.

5. Two parts worm castings; one part each compost or humus, vermiculite, and perlite. Needs little initial fertilization, but must have supplementation during flowering.

6. Two parts potting soil; one part vermiculite; one part perlite. Has organic materials for buffers and promotes drainage.

ADDITIVES

A few things can be added to mixes to enhance them in one way or another. Here are some that gardeners sometimes add.

Hydrated lime contains calcium, which plants use in large amounts. Not all fertilizers contain this element, so adding about $1/4$ teaspoon per 6" pot of mix (one teaspoon per gallon of mix) will supply the plants with adequate amounts. Experienced gardeners may have recipes including additives or nutrients not listed here.

Polymer crystals are sold at local plant stores and nurseries. They have tremendous water-holding capacity and expand from small flakes to 100 times their volume when they come in contact with water. They should be used sparingly. Some growers claim that as well as increasing time between watering, they increase the growth rate and the general vigor of the plant. Some commercial potting mixes contain these crystals.

Time-release fertilizer can be used to maintain the plants with only supplemental feeding through the water. These fertilizers are mixed into the planting medium as it is prepared. They are convenient to use. They come in various formulas with various time periods for release. Use mixes with a release period of three to four months and a bloom formula (see Chapter 15, "Nutrients, Fertilizers and pH").

PREPARING THE MIX

The first consideration in preparing a mix is always safety. Many of the ingredients create dust when they are moved around. For this reason, it is advisable to moisten the ingredients before working with them. This can be accomplished by opening the package and wetting the mix with a sprinkling can. The water should contain a wetting agent to break surface tension. A teaspoon of dishwashing liquid per gallon of water works well.

If they are using vermiculite or perlite, which are very prone to release dust, growers work in an area with good ventilation, wear rubber gloves or garden gloves and long sleeved clothing, and use a respirator. However, the best way to deal with this problem is to prevent the dust by prewetting the medium as described above.

It is easier to get the ingredients mixed consistently when the medium is prepared in small batches.

PREPARING THE CONTAINERS

New containers require no cleaning. However, used ones should be washed thoroughly so that any parasites or infectious agents are removed. It is not necessary to buy horticultural pots, but they are generally easier to use than other containers because their graduated sides make it easy to slide out the medium and rootball. Once the mix has been prepared, it is time to fill the containers with planting mix. Using a container or a small shovel, each pot is filled with mix to about one inch from the top. The containers should be placed in a tray or, even better, on blocks so that the pots are off the ground and will be out of any contact with water that drains from them.

CHAPTER 7

HYDROPONIC GARDENING

Hydroponics is the method of cultivating plants in an inert medium and supplying all the nutrients using a water-nutrient solution. It has many advantages over most soil systems; it usually results in higher yields. Most hydroponic systems are fairly easy to set up and require little maintenance afterwards. They eliminate the need for dealing with potting mixes and are very clean-looking. However, they are more finicky than potting mixes.

TYPES OF SYSTEMS

Over the years, people have invented many different kinds of hydroponic systems. These fall into six basic categories: wick, reservoir, flood (ebb-and-flow), drip, nutrient film, and water.

There are hundreds of books on hydroponics and the systems can be quite complicated. However, it is not difficult to make a system fairly inexpensively. Small systems can also be purchased that require little or no assembly and work quite well.

We will start by describing the simplest systems and move to the more complex, which are still quite easy to understand and to install.

RESERVOIR SYSTEMS

These use regular planting containers to hold plants, but the pots sit in trays that hold water, so the roots are partially submerged.

Reservoir systems are very easy to make. Containers are placed in individual trays, or groups of containers in large trays such as dish or restaurant trays, larger trays that are sold in housewares and indoor garden stores, or even kiddie pools. Four-foot-round plastic kiddie pools cover an area of 12 square feet. Five-foot pools cover just under 20 square feet. Either size is convenient to use and can hold an entire garden.

These systems are available commercially in individual containers with a special clay-pellet planting medium. The Luwassa system, which is widely used in Europe, also has an indicator to let you know when to water. In the U.S., Hydrofarm manufactures "Emily's Garden" based on this principle.

Most American gardening books caution that roots sitting in water may be damaged. However, as long as the roots come in contact with oxygen as well as water and nutrients, their needs are met. Some manufacturers, concerned about this, add a fish-tank bubbler to the tray. This circulates the water so that it absorbs more oxygen.

This system works best with hydrocorn, a horticultural clay pellet that absorbs moisture through capillary action. The clay balls maintain large air spaces between pieces. Capillary action, the same process by which water climbs up a paper napkin, keeps the entire root system supplied with moisture. The bottom half of each container is filled with hydrocorn, then the container is filled to the top with a mixture of perlite and vermiculite.

Once the pots are filled with the medium, the tray is filled to a depth of about 20% with water-nutrient solution. A tray with pots eight inches high should hold one-and-one-half to two inches of water; with twelve-inch containers, the tray should hold about two-and-one-half inches of water. The medium uses capillary action to replace water as moisture leaves the medium. Thus, the medium stays at a constant moisture level unless the reservoir runs out.

The water in the tray should be replaced as it is used so that it stays at a fairly constant level. The system can be automated using a bucket as a reservoir and a float valve such as the ones used in toilets. When the water level falls, the valve opens, filling the tray to the desired level.

This garden is easy to operate, has no moving parts or water, and almost takes care of itself. It is an ideal system for a small garden and can be set up very quickly and easily.

WICK SYSTEMS

These work using capillary action to draw water from a reservoir to the container through 3/8" nylon cord, which wicks the water up to the potting mix. These were the very first hydroponic units I ever used and they work quite well. In fact, I sometimes still use them to grow plants, both indoors and outdoors. Because they use capillary action to self-water, they keep the containers at an even moisture level.

This system uses the same equipment as the reservoir system, with two additions: 3/8" nylon wick to draw the water up to the containers and a platform to elevate the container above the water.

To create the system, a nylon cord is run outward through the drainage holes in the container so that the two ends trail out of the holes and are long enough to reach the bottom of the reservoir. A container with four holes can use two wicks. Then the containers are filled with a medium that includes some vermiculite on the bottom to promote the capillary action. Almost any potting mix will work in this system. The first one I used was composed only of vermiculite. Many growers use a one-to-one mix of vermiculite and perlite.

Planting containers are placed in trays holding either single containers or groups of them. One gardener grew two plants each in five-gallon-bucket wick systems. Each unit consisted of two buckets. The bottom one was the reservoir and was not modified. The plant container had four holes drilled in it and wicks ran through them extending down to the reservoir container. He placed an eight-inch Styrofoam block between the containers so they wouldn't lock together. The planting buckets were filled with a mix of vermiculite, perlite, compost, and peat moss. The reservoir bucket was filled with six inches of water.

Wick systems are extremely easy to make, but are also sold commercially. They are easy to set up and use, since no moving water or parts are involved. They can be used to grow large numbers of plants. Large trays hold large numbers of containers. Watering is extremely easy.

EBB-AND-FLOW SYSTEMS

Sometimes called flood-and-drain systems, these consist of a water-proof table with side walls. The table is filled periodically with water from a reservoir. Once the table is filled, irrigating the planting medium, the pump is turned off automatically, allowing the water to drain.

Small systems are available from many hydroponic companies. Using one of these may be more convenient than gathering all the parts for just one or two systems.

Of all active-water hydroponic systems, ebb-and-flow systems are the least expensive to set up and the easiest to maintain. They require little plumbing. Since they use only large-diameter tubing, clogging and other problems rarely occur.

The size of the system, its design, and the container used for it is open to imagination. All units consist of a tray or container that holds the plants, a water reservoir, a planting unit, a timer, a pump, and tubing from the pump to the planting unit.

A simple unit can be built using a plastic or plastic-lined wooden tray at least five inches deep. It should be placed over a plastic reservoir and have drainage holes with a cover that allows the water to drain slowly. An over-flow drain on the side wall can help prevent accidental flooding. The reservoir should contain a minimum of two gallons of water per square foot of growing space.

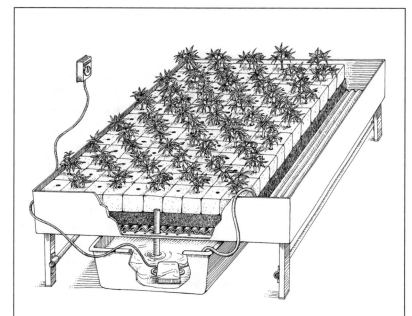

Ebb-and-Flow System

This ebb-and-flow table is 4'✕4' with 8" high sides. 4" rockwool cubes are placed on top of 4'✕8"✕3" rockwool slabs to allow them to grow more extensive root systems. The slabs sit on top of corrugated plastic sheets that carry excess water toward the drainage holes at the lower end of the table. The drainage tube acts as an overflow valve in case water is pumped in too quickly.

The pump is controlled by a timer. When the pump turns on, it fills the tray to the level of the overflow valve. The water drains from the side drain holes at a slower rate than it comes from the pump. When the pump stops, all the water drains out.

Ideally, the timer is set to turn the pump off soon after the water reaches its maximum level. Only electronic timers can be set for the three- to six-minute increments it usually takes to fill a tray. The more common analog timers have minimum increments of 15 minutes or

30 minutes. If you have an analog timer, leave it on for the minimum amount of time possible.

Square trays suitable for ebb-and-flow gardens are sold in housewares stores and indoor garden shops. Commercial flower and bedding growers often use trays or tables to grow plants in individual containers. The containers usually contain peat-based or bark-based potting mix. Six-inch-tall containers receive only about three inches of water, but the water travels throughout the medium through capillary action.

The plants are watered from once every three days to several times daily, depending on the planting medium, the size of the plant, and the temperature, since more water is used when it is warm. The mix is constantly kept moist. Marijuana growers can use exactly the same technique.

Mediums that can be used directly in the trays, or in containers in the trays, include gravel, hydrostone, polyurethane slabs, and rockwool. The frequency of irrigation must be adjusted to the size of the plant and the container, the medium's water-holding capacity, and light and temperature. A planting medium mix may, in a spacious container, need water only every day or two. Hydrocorn is irrigated four to six times a day or more.

I recently saw a modified "Ebb" system. Six-inch-wide containers were filled with a mixture of two parts each perlite and vermiculite and one part worm-castings. The containers were placed in trays. Using a bucket or hose, water-nutrient solution was added to the trays until a one inch level remained after the containers were saturated. The remaining inch of water-nutrient solution was absorbed within a day. Water was never drained, only added. The system worked very well.

Ebb-and-flow systems are often used in commercial agriculture, because they are relatively foolproof and are easy to maintain. There are no small emitters to clog; the water moves through larger pipes and then drains.

DRIP SYSTEMS

These systems use a pump to drip water through an emitter onto the top of the medium. The water percolates through the medium, then drains back to the reservoir and is ready to be recirculated.

Drip systems are easy to set up. Water is pumped from a reservoir, which is usually located below the growing area, to individual drip emitters, each feeding one plant. The plants can either be in trays or in individual containers. The water drains from the containers and runs back into the reservoir. The reservoir should hold about one gallon of water for every square foot of growing space.

Hydroponic companies sell many ingeniously designed drip systems. Some units recirculate water in individual containers, each of which holds one plant. Other units recirculate water from a central reservoir. Both designs work well.

Commercial units are very convenient, but homemade systems are not hard to construct. A simple but very effective unit consists of a table with raised sides, at a slight tilt to promote drainage. The tilt should be at a ratio of 1–40. This works out to one-third inch per running foot. One side of a 40-inch-long table should be one inch lower than the other side.

The planting containers rest on the table. They usually range from six to twelve inches, depending on the plant size desired. Flexible tubing, $1/2$" or $3/4$" in diameter, is attached to a small submersible pump in the reservoir under the table. Thinner, $1/4$" diameter tubing, referred to as spaghetti tubing, branches from the central tube. Emitters, which regulate water flow, are attached to each of the lines. Emitters that are rated at one gallon per hour (gph) are usually the best.

Water is pumped from the reservoir, through the tubing and emitter to the top of the pot. It percolates down through the medium to the table where it is collected into a tube or gutter and flows back into the reservoir.

The containers can be placed on a flat surface, but corrugated plastic is sometimes used as a tabletop to hold individual containers because it promotes drainage so well.

An inexpensive, very easy drip system can be made using a kiddie pool and a pallet or other support to raise the planting containers. The pool is the reservoir. Water flows from the pump, submerged in the reservoir, to the drip emitters, percolates through the containers, and then drips back directly into the pool. In one version of this system, containers holding hydrostone are raised, but the water submerges the bottom 20% of the container, as in the reservoir system.

Regular planting containers or plastic trays with sides that are two inches or higher can be used to make drip systems. The planting container must provide easy drainage.

Tubing, pressure regulators, spaghetti line, and emitters are all available at garden shops as well as indoor garden stores.

NUTRIENT FILM TECHNIQUE

This technique uses a constant spray or flow of water to provide water and nutrient to the roots. The theory is that by optimizing conditions for the roots they will perform at peak efficiency, promoting faster growth.

Researchers have come to the conclusion that for many plants, including marijuana, this is achieved by coating the roots with a thin film of water. This provides the roots with constantly changing water so that the microenvironment around the root is never depleted of nutrients. At the same time, there is an extremely high surface-to-mass ratio so high levels of oxygen are dissolved in the water as it is relieved of CO_2.

There are several ways to create an NFT system. The easiest and least technical consists of a drip system, filled with pebbles or hydrostone, in which the drippers are constantly working. A thin film of water constantly flows over the stone.

A more exotic commercial unit consists of tubes in which holes have been cut to accommodate small cups. Each cup holds a single plant. Inside, the tube emitters are constantly directing a spray at the containers, creating a film of water around the roots.

When these units work they produce large crops. However, the failure rate is high because they have no redundancy or "safety net." They are affected more than other units by temperature fluctuation and must be monitored constantly to make sure all the emitters are working and the unit is functioning at 100%. I do not think these are good units for the closet cultivator.

PLANTING MEDIUMS

Hydroponic growers have a choice of planting mediums to use. A commercial unit will usually come complete with some medium, but with homemade units, gardeners must make their own choices.

The following mineral ingredients are virtually inert; they have no nutrients and don't interact with the water-nutrient solution.

FOAM RUBBER

Polyurethane foam (P.U. foam) is available in some indoor gardening shops; it is recycled from foam scrap. It is inert and does not release noxious chemicals. It holds both water and air. Foam can be used in several ways. Pieces of foam, from pea size to about 1/2", can be used as an ingredient in planting mixes with vermiculite, perlite, or bark-or peat moss-based mixes.

Foam rubber can also be used alone. Solid eight inch strips of foam are designed to fit into European one-meter hydro trays, which are readily available. Manufacturers claim that the material can be used for several years. It is suitable for use as part of a mix in reservoir, wick, or drip systems, and can also be used alone in drip systems or ebb-and-flow systems.

GRAVEL

Gravel is composed of small stones. It promotes drainage and holds water on its surface while providing large air spaces. Not all gravel is the same. Make sure to get a non-calcium-based stone that is inert and has neutral pH.

Unlike hydrostone, which absorbs water and moves it up through the medium, gravel holds water between the pieces but does not promote capillary action. Pearl-sized pieces, one-eighth to one-quarter inch, are suitable for use in mixes. Larger pieces can be used alone in drip systems or for total immersion in ebb-and-flow units.

HORICULTURAL CLAY PELLETS

Also called hydrocorn or hydrostone, this material is very popular because it is easy to work with and inert. Its round shape makes it easy to dig into and plant roots pull out easily. It also lasts indefinitely and can easily be cleaned or sterilized. The round fired-clay pellets absorb water through capillary action and provide lots of air space between the stones. It is suitable for use in all systems.

LAVA CHIPS

These have an irregular surface that holds water in the surface crevices, and also promotes capillary action. I have used them for planting for many years in all kinds of systems. They have several disadvantages, compared with clay pellets. First of all, lava is much heavier. It is also much harder to pot with because it doesn't pour well. In addition, it should be tested by growing a trial plant to be sure that it doesn't leach minerals that can harm the plants, which occasionally happens. It does have a few advantages: it has an irregular pitted surface which allows more space for roots; it also holds more moisture because capillary action is greater.

PERLITE

This is an extremely lightweight, puffed volcanic glass. It is inert and can be reused as long as it is cleaned. It has a pitted surface that holds water particles while allowing air spaces between the pieces. It is hard to the touch and does not break down. It comes in several sizes, but only the coarse or medium size should be used. Dry perlite is very dusty. The bag should be watered before the material is removed to avoid inhaling the dust. It is wise to use a respirator mask, as well.

Perlite can be used as an ingredient in planting mixes or it can be used alone. It is suitable as an ingredient in mixes used as the top part in a reservoir system, as an ingredient in mixes for wick systems, and alone or as an ingredient in drip systems. It is lighter than water so it cannot be used in ebb-and-flow systems. Since it consists of small particles, in recirculating drip systems the water should be filtered through a screen or through sand as it returns to the reservoir, to prevent plumbing clogs. Perlite is often used with vermiculite in drip and wick systems.

SAND

Sand promotes drainage and keeps mixes from caking. Both horticultural and construction sand can be used, but avoid limestone sand. Sand is very heavy and has largely been replaced by perlite and vermiculite. However, it can be used to weight the containers if there is a chance that they may tip over. Sand can be used as a minor ingredient in reservoir, wick, drip, and ebb-and-flow systems. Because of its heavy weight and small size, it tends to migrate to the bottom of the mix over a period of time.

ROCKWOOL

Rockwool is the most popular planting medium in Europe and is very popular in the U.S. It is composed of fine strands of spun basalt rock and looks a lot like glass wool. It's basically the same material that is used for insulation, without the chemical additives and with slightly different qualities. It is pulled or cut and added to mixes. Its most popular forms are cubes, blocks, and slabs.

Rockwool is alkaline. It raises the pH of the water and should be soaked in a 5.5 pH acid solution to neutralize it before it is used. It should be prepared with caution. The fine strands weave their way into clothing and irritate the skin. These thin strands also break off and float in the air. They are then easily breathed in and lodge in the lungs. To avoid problems, rockwool should be thoroughly moistened before use, the user should wear a mask, and cover his/her body. Using rubber gloves and disposable clothing is also recommended.

Rockwool cubes come in many sizes. One-and-one-half-inch-square cubes are often used to start seeds or root cuttings. Four-inch cubes are used to continue growth and if large plants are desired, these cubes are placed on eight-inch-wide slabs. When one piece of rockwool is placed on another, the roots in the older piece grow into the new one.

VERMICULITE

Vermiculite is made up of the mineral, mica, which is "popped" using heat. It absorbs many times its weight in water, while promoting drainage. It is very lightweight and comes in various grades. The fine size is used for seed starting, cuttings and plants in small containers. Medium or large pieces are used for most other sized containers. Dry vermiculite is dusty and may contain small amounts of asbestos, but it is safe and convenient to use once it is moistened. It is suitable for use alone or as an ingredient in the top part mix in reservoir systems, and alone or as an ingredient in wick and drip systems. Like perlite, vermiculite consists of small pieces that can clog small pipes. The water should be filtered as it re-enters the reservoir to prevent plumbing problems.

PLANTING MIXES

Many of the ingredients described in the hydroponic section can be mixed together to create a suitable planting medium. Some growers add organic ingredients such as compost, humus, peat moss, or worm castings to the mix to promote microbial activity and act as a buffer. These mixes usually have vermiculite and perlite as their main ingredients.

Peat moss and bark mediums are also suitable ingredients for wick and drip systems. They hold much more water than other mixes and need irrigation much less frequently. In addition, they "buffer" the fertilizers so that there is less chance of failure due to improper fertilizing. Microorganisms living in the organic matter tie up excess nutrients as they use the nutrients for their life processes. As roots use up the nutrients remaining in the mix, more gradually become available as the microorganisms release them.

PLANTING MIX RECIPES

1. One part each (by volume) vermiculite and perlite. This is good for the top part of a reservoir mix, or for wick or drip systems.

2. Two parts each vermiculite and perlite, 1 part compost, humus, or worm castings. This can also be used for the top part of reservoir mix, or for wick or drip systems.

3. One part each vermiculite, perlite, clean sand, small bark chips, worm castings, bark-based planting mix. This is used for wick or drip systems.

4. One part each rockwool, perlite, and worm castings. This is used for wick or drip systems.

CHAPTER 8

LIGHT

Plants use light as energy to fuel photosynthesis, a process in which water and carbon dioxide are converted to sugar. Sugar is the basic building block of all plants. Without light, green plants have no way of producing food and they die.

By chemically twisting and tweaking the sugar molecule, plants form carbohydrates, which are more complex molecules. With the addition of nitrogen, amino acids are formed. These group together to form proteins, the building blocks for tissue.

Closet gardens require electric lights to power the plants. Since marijuana is a sun-loving plant, it requires a high intensity of light to grow and thrive.

LIGHT SPECTRUMS AND PHOTOSYNTHESIS

To produce chlorophyll, plants need light from specific spectrums-mainly red and blue light. This is called the chlorophyll spectrum. Chlorophyll uses a slightly different spectrum of light to power photosynthesis, the process that results in sugar production.

Plants use red and blue light most efficiently, but they also use orange and, to a lesser extent, yellow light. Plants are continually growing as well as producing new chlorophyll, so both spectrums of light are continually being used by the plant. Plants reflect green light rather than absorbing and using it.

Each source of light has a characteristic spectrum that is caused by varying wavelengths of light. To our eyes, midday summer sunlight looks neutral, incandescent lights have a reddish tint, fluorescents vary in spectrum according to their type, metal halide (MH) lamps have a blue coolness to them, and high-pressure sodium (HPS) lamps look pink-amber.

TYPES OF LIGHTS
FLUORESCENTS

Until the early 1980s, most indoor growers used fluorescent tubes for budding as well as cloning and early vegetative growth. These tubes have tremendous advantages over screw-in incandescent lights. A fluorescent emits about three- to five-times as much light as an incandescent of the same wattage.

Standard fluorescents, such as the four-foot tubes, have their limitations. Light is emitted over a large area, the entire surface of the tube, so it is not concentrated. The tubes are bulky, so only a limited amount of light can be delivered to a given area. The fixtures are usually placed within inches of the plants, so that the light does not spread and become less intense. When the light fixtures are hung, they are hard to manipulate, making it more difficult to tend the garden.

Fluorescents have their uses. They are the best lights to use for cloning and early vegetative growth and are sometimes used in small gardens. They are no longer limited to bulky fixtures, so they can be used to supplement other light.

Housewares stores sell many types of screw-in fluorescents for incandescent fixtures. These bulbs come in several shapes, including circles and U shapes. They are convenient because they are compact and can easily be placed around the garden.

Gardens lit by fluorescents require an input of at least 30 watts per square foot to produce vigorous plants and good bud. This comes to three tubes for each foot of width if regular fluorescent four-foot or eight-foot tubes are used. With the new screw-in fluorescents, which use compact tubes, the lamps can be placed close together to provide higher intensity.

The inner surface of each fluorescent tube is covered with a phosphor that glows when it is stimulated by the flow of electrons through it. Fluorescent tubes are named for the spectrum of light that they emit. For specific periods of plant growth, some spectrums are more conducive to growth than others.

Fluorescents for Rooting and Vegetative Growth

During the rooting and vegetative growth stages, plants grow shorter, stockier stems when they are grown under a "cool" lamp such as cool white shop-lite, cool white, or other tubes with "cool" in their names, which denotes that they are high in the blue spectrum.

Probably the best fluorescent light for cloning and vegetative growth is the GE Chroma 5000,® or a tube with similar specifications. It is very high in blue-spectrum light and is about 20% brighter than standard tubes using the same amount of electricity.

While cuttings are being rooted, only one tube per foot of width, (about nine watts per foot squared), is needed to maintain the plants. Once the plants have roots, they require more light to grow compactly. While they are still in the vegetative growth stage, they can get by on 20 watts per foot squared, but grow faster if they receive about 30 watts.

"Full spectrum" fluorescents, such as Vita-Lites,™ emit a light balance close to the sun's spectrum. Many growers swear by these lights and use them for all stages of growth.

During vegetative growth, avoid warm white tubes, tubes with "warm" in their names, or tubes that emit a warm glow. These will promote stretching and premature flowering.

Some manufacturers produce fluorescent grow tubes formulated to provide a light spectrum similar to the chlorophyll synthesis or photosynthesis spectrum or a compromise between them.

Grow tubes can be used for cultivation, alone or in combination with other tubes. Although they produce less total light, some of them emit more light that is usable by the plants than standard tubes. During vegetative growth, use the wide-spectrum grow tubes or tubes with a pink (rather than purplish) light. These have more blue and less red than the others, promoting stocky stems and short internodes.

Fluorescents for Flowering

During flowering, the plants can use a lot more red light than they can during vegetative growth. Fluorescent tubes suitable for this stage of growth are warm white and warm white deluxe tubes, fluorescents with "incandescent" spectrums, and compact lights with a warm or reddish glow.

The GE Chroma 3000® or a tube with similar specifications is an excellent four-foot or eight-foot tube that promotes flowering and fast ripening. However, some screw-in fluorescents have more red which promotes flowering and ripening.

Caring for Fluorescents

As fluorescent tubes age, they become less efficient. On the average, they lose 25% of the light they were rated for after a year of use. They should be replaced so that the garden stays bright. Lights that are turned on and off a lot wear out faster. Three-inch to six-inch sections on both sides of the tube dull out from deposits after a short term of use. The effective length of a four-foot tube is three feet, eight inches and that of an eight-foot tube is seven feet.

Fluorescent Light Reflectors

Fluorescent tubes come in many lengths, but the two most commonly used by indoor gardeners are four-foot and eight-foot. They are convenient and more efficient than other sizes.

Most fluorescent fixtures are poorly designed, with no baffles between the individual tubes to reflect light downward. They lose up to 40% of the light. Instead, if possible, the tubes should be mounted on a reflector with baffles between the tubes so that light is directed downward to the garden. A good reflector keeps the light loss down to 20%. These fixtures cost a little more, but save money in the long run because of the light they save.

An alternative is to use tubes with reflective surfaces, which are made by several manufacturers. Housewares and lighting stores do not usually carry them, but will special-order them.

HIGH-INTENSITY DISCHARGE LAMPS

High-intensity discharge lamps (HIDs) are more convenient and more efficient than fluorescents. Low-wattage HIDs are sometimes sold in housewares stores and are often convenient to use in small gardens. High-wattage systems are sold in grow stores and garden shops.

HID lights are powered by heavy ballasts (400W–28lbs., 1000W–40lbs.), which are usually connected to the light by a long electrical wire. Some 400-watt HID systems are manufactured with the ballast built into the same housing as the reflector. These lamps are harder to move around and are usually considered for lighting only if they are to be permanently mounted.

HID lighting systems are much more convenient to use than fluorescents because the lamps are not nearly as bulky as banks of fluorescents. HIDs also have higher wattages and are more efficient at producing light than fluorescents.

METAL HALIDE LAMPS

Metal halide, or MH, lamps emit a white light that looks slightly bluish. They are used to light stadiums, convention centers, and other large areas where a natural-looking light is desired. They are used for rooting and vegetative growth by many gardeners. Some gardeners use them in conjunction with high-pressure sodium lamps during flowering.

Aside from the low-wattage lamps sold in housewares stores, MH lamps come in 175-, 250-, 400-, and 1000-watt sizes. Each lamp comes with its own ballast.

High-wattage systems are more efficient than low-wattage ones. MH lamps have an efficiency of 35 to 50%. The higher the wattage, the more efficient the bulb. Moving the lamp and reflector is easy, since they are fairly light.

HIGH-PRESSURE SODIUM LAMPS

High pressure sodium, or HPS, lamps emit a pink or amber light. They are used to illuminate parking lots and other areas where the color of the light is not important. HPS lamps are more efficient than MH lamps. They can be used by themselves and will promote faster growth than MH bulbs during both vegetative growth and flowering. Combinations of bulbs are not required, because the HPS has all the light spectrums necessary for healthy growth.

Under HPS lamps, some varieties of indoor plants grow flowers while in the vegetative stage. This will not hurt the plant, and it will start flowering more quickly once it is forced to flower.

HPS lamps come in 150-, 400-, and 1000-watt sizes and have an efficiency of 50 to 55%. They also come with their own ballasts.

HPS vs. MH LAMPS

HPS lamps emit more light in the red spectrum than MH lamps. The red spectrum is used more efficiently than the blue by plants for photosynthesis. However, both lamps produce high levels of light in the critical wave lengths.

HPS lamps produce more growth because they emit more light as well as a higher percentage in the red spectrum, resulting in more energy that the plants can use to power photosynthesis.

MH lamps do have their uses. The high percentage of blue light they emit promotes rooting and stocky plants. Many growers use these lights for the early stages of growth and switch to HPS lamps during the later stages. However, in an informal comparison of the Chroma 5000 lamps and MH, the fluorescents produced more successful rootings and stockier, healthier plants during early growth.

Some gardeners and garden-store salespeople maintain that combinations of MH and HPS lights produce the fastest growth. My observation is that HPS lamps by themselves produce the fastest growth. Plants grown under HPS lamps exhibit a little more stem etiolation (stretching) and ripen up to a week later. This is more than compensated for by a considerably larger crop.

This chart shows how much light each lamp emits, its lumen output per 100 watts, and the area it covers adequately.

WATTS	NO. OF LUMENS EMITTED	NO. OF LUMENS PER 100 WATTS	SQ. FEET ILLUMINATED
100W Incandescent	1,750	1,750	N/A
4' Fluorescent (CW-40W)	2,960	7,400	1–2
8' Fluorescent (CW-40W)	5,800	7,400	2–4
MH 175W	14,000	8,000	3–6
MH 400W	40,000	10,000	8–16
MH 1000W	125,000	12,500	25–50
HPS 100W	9,500	9,500	2–5
HPS 150W	16,000	10,600	3–8
HPS 400W	50,000	12,500	8–20
HPS 1000W	140,000	14,000	25–50

Because of the ease and convenience of operating HID lamps and because of their terrific efficiency, they are recommended for most indoor gardens.

LIGHT INTENSITY

Gardens should receive between 3000 and 5000 lumens (per square foot), although plants will grow under as little as 1000 lumens. The brighter the light, the faster and the higher the yield of the garden. When plants receive high light levels, they grow stocky with profuse flowering and dense colas. Given less light, the plants stretch more and produce looser flowers.

The following chart shows the approximate amount of light received by gardens of various sizes using a very efficient reflector. Twenty percent of light emitted has been deducted from the total to correct for reflector inefficiency and light that never reaches the garden. Light is never distributed evenly, so some parts of the garden get more light than others.

NUMBER OF KILOWATT HOURS USED AT DIFFERENT WATTAGES

	NUMBER OF HOURS DAILY			NUMBER OF HOURS MONTHLY		
	12	18	24	12	18	242
175 Watts	2.1	3.15	4.2	63	95	126
250 Watts	3.0	4.5	6.0	90	135	180
400 Watts	4.8	7.2	9.6	144	216.0	288.0
1000 Watts	12	18	24	360	540	720

LIGHTS AND REFLECTORS

Sunlight comes from a distant source, so light rays striking a small portion of planet Earth (say, a garden ten feet wide) are virtually parallel. Also, their intensity does not decrease over the length of a plant three feet tall.

Light emitted from tubes or lamps travels in all directions. As the distance from the lamp increases, intensity of the light decreases. It is not that light is lost, just that the same amount of light is spread over a larger area.

HID lamps and reflectors come in two configurations. The lamps are held either vertically or horizontally.

Horizontally held lamps direct most of the light downward because the light is emitted along the length of the lamp. Only a small reflector is required to beam the rest of the light downward.

Vertical lights emit most of their light horizontally. To reach the garden, the light must be reflected downward using a large, bulky reflector. Manufacturers have developed elaborate and innovative hoods, but they do not have the light-delivery efficiency of a horizontal lamp.

Horizontally held lamps have several other advantages over verticals. They take less vertical space, and the reflectors are much less bulky. All in all, horizontally held lamps are the best configuration for the closet garden.

Aluminum reflectors deliver the most light, more than white ones. Stainless steel reflectors absorb some spectrums of light and should not be used.

In his book, *Gardening Indoors with H.I.D. Lights*, George Van Patten reported on his experiments, which showed that the amount of light that gets to the garden varies tremendously depending upon the reflector. He found that the most efficient appliances were Hydrofarm's and Superior Growers' dual-wing parabolic reflectors.

COSTS

In initial purchase price, HPS systems are the most expensive of all lighting units. MH lamps are a little cheaper, and fluorescents the cheapest of all. However, this takes into account only the initial outlay. If we calculate the cost per unit of light produced, the positions are reversed: HPS lamps become the cheapest, followed by MH lamps. The fluorescents become much more expensive.

COST IN CENTS TO GENERATE 1000 LUMENS FROM VARIOUS LAMPS.

LAMP	OUTPUT IN LUMENS	OUTPUT PER 100 WATTS	COST PER KILOWATT HOUR OF ELECTRICITY			
			8¢	10¢	12¢	15¢
100W Incandescent	1,750	1,750	4.5	5.7	6.8	8.5
40W CW FL	2,960	7,400	1.1	1.3	1.6	2.0
175W MH	14,000	8,000	1.0	1.2	1.5	1.9
400W MH	40,000	10,000	.8	1.0	1.2	1.5
1000W MH	125,000	12,500	.6	.8	1.0	1.2
100W HPS	9,500	9,500	.8	1.0	1.3	1.6
400W HPS	50,000	12,500	.6	.8	1.0	1.2
1000W HPS	140,000	14,000	.6	.7	.9	1.1

The ultimate question is: How much does the electricity cost monthly? The handy chart below shows what a person can expect the bill for lighting the garden to be. In addition to lights, the garden may use electricity for heating, cooling, moving water, fans, and other accessories.

COST PER KW	1¢	5¢	10¢
# of Hours On		175 Watt Lamp	
12	$.63	$3.15	$6.30
18	$.95	$4.75	$9.50
24	$1.26	$6.30	$12.60
# of Hours On		250 Watt Lamp	
12	$.90	$4.50	$9.00
18	$1.35	$6.75	$13.50
24	$1.80	$9.00	$18.00
# of Hours On		400 Watt Lamp	
12	$1.44	$7.20	$14.40
18	$2.16	$10.80	$21.60
24	$2.88	$14.40	$28.80
# of Hours On		1000 Watt Lamp	
12	$3.60	$18.00	$36.00
18	$5.40	$27.00	$54.00
24	$7.20	$36.00	$72.00

LIGHTING ACCESSORIES

Outdoors, plants receive light from many directions. Over the course of the day, the sun bathes plants in light starting in the east and traveling west. Leaves shaded during part of the day are under full sun at other times. When there is some cloud cover, the light is dispersed, so leaves are more evenly bathed in light.

Indoors, using a single stationary light, some plant parts are always shaded while others are always lit. With a light in the center of the garden, plants closer to the source receive brighter light than those at the periphery.

LIGHT MOVERS

Light movers were invented to solve light distribution problems. The mover carries the lamp over a fixed course so that the entire garden comes directly under the light part of the time. Some movers shuttle the lamps quickly, so, that the light passes over the garden in less than a minute. Other movers take more time to traverse the course. Both types improve light distribution in the garden. As a result, the plants grow at an even rate. The plants do not stretch the way they do under a stationary light. Instead, they grow straighter, with more symmetry.

The rotating units are most effective in block-shaped areas, while the shuttles, which go back and forth, are most effective in rectangular spaces.

REFLECTIVE MATERIAL

Electrically generated light is expensive, so any that is generated should be conserved. Efficient indoor gardens use reflective material to shoot back light that strays out of the perimeter. Growers cover walls with flat white paint, aluminum foil or metallic gift wrap, Mylar, white polyethylene plastic, or Styrofoam.

Flat white paint diffracts the light so that it is distributed more evenly throughout the garden. Some greenhouse white paint is formulated with titanium for maximum reflectivity.

Aluminum foil is very reflective and inexpensive. The best way to use it is to line walls and surfaces with it, rather than to leave it hanging. The heavy-duty 18-inch width is very convenient. Use the dull side, since it diffracts the light. Metallic wrapping paper is very reflective, inexpensive, and easier to use than aluminum foil. It comes in 26-inch to 30-inch widths, in 100-foot and 500-foot rolls. The aluminized section is backed by paper, so it doesn't wrinkle much and it can easily be replaced if it gets dirty. Both of these materials are totally opaque, so they can be used as total light barriers.

Mylar is a metallic plastic that is sold at garden shops and other stores. It comes in wide rolls, so it can be installed very quickly. It loses its metallic coating when it is splashed with some chemicals. While it has very high reflectivity, it is not opaque, so a lit garden can be seen through the material.

White polyethylene plastic is inexpensive, fairly reflective, easy to install, and very washable. It comes in many widths and presents a water barrier as well as reflectivity. It is a preferred material. Sometimes it is available in white on one side and black on the other, which makes it opaque. It can be used to construct a "room" in a much larger space by hanging or tacking it on a frame. It is easy to work with and can be installed quickly.

White Styrofoam insulation boards are extremely reflective and very easy to use. Because they are solid, they can be hung from ceilings with string to create spaces, tacked to a wall or light frame, or leaned against a garden apparatus. They are lightweight and easy to move, and can be restored to their original brightness by washing them with household cleaner.

CHAPTER 9

CARBON DIOXIDE

Carbon dioxide (CO_2) is a colorless, odorless gas found in the air. Under normal circumstances, including the conditions growers deal with, CO_2 is harmless. It is neither poisonous nor combustible. Each molecule consists of one atom of carbon and two atoms of oxygen. Carbon dioxide is often generated in the home. When a stove or water heater burns gas, it produces heat, water vapor, and CO_2.

Plants use CO_2 as a raw material during the process of photosynthesis. In the air, the concentration of CO_2 is about 350 parts-per-million (ppm). When the level in the air goes down to 200 ppm, photosynthesis stops and does not resume until the concentration rises. Therefore, the availability of CO_2 to the plant can be a limiting factor in photosynthesis and plant growth.

Higher concentrations of CO_2, 1000 to 2000 ppm, provide several benefits to the garden. Most important, they can increase the growth rate by up to 300%, although increases in most gardens are under 100%. This results in a larger harvest in less time. Plants growing in a CO_2-enriched space also grow thicker, more vigorous stems.

CO_2 can be used during both vegetative and flowering cycles. The gas can be shut off a week before ripening for two reasons: there isn't much growth taking place and it is possible that the gas hinders production of some of the odors. Since photosynthesis takes place only during the lit period, plants do not use CO_2 during the dark period and the space does not need enrichment then.

Carbon dioxide is much cheaper to provide than lighting, so CO_2 enrichment is a very economical way to increase the rate of plant growth. Brighter gardens can use higher concentrations of CO_2 than gardens with less light. Gardens lit by fluorescents or HIDs with less than 25 watts of light per square foot can use up to 1000 ppm CO_2. Gardens using 25 to 40 watts per square foot can use 1500 ppm. Plants growing under 40 watts or more per square foot can use 2000 ppm.

Besides increasing growth rate, CO_2 provides the garden with another advantage: plants in enriched atmospheres grow faster at higher temperatures, the low 80s rather than the mid-70s. The result is that less energy needs to be put into maintaining proper temperature.

CO_2 IN THE UNENRICHED GARDEN

Even if the garden is not enriched with CO_2, the gas must be constantly replaced as it's used. Keeping the door or curtain of a small garden space open helps tremendously, because a whole side of the grow space is exposed to external air. This keeps the ppm level close to that of the surrounding atmosphere. An open door in a large room gives a much smaller interface ratio because the percentage of the perimeter serving as a vent is much smaller.

The addition of fans exchanging air between the garden space and the outside helps to keep the CO_2 level near atmospheric levels. For a small garden, a window box fan can provide adequate air exchange. Larger gardens require more elaborate ventilation. An intake fan blowing in fresh air is usually placed near the bottom of the garden. An exhaust fan is placed in the ceiling or near the top of a wall.

CO_2 ENRICHMENT

Ventilation and fans replace depleted with fresh air, but they don't provide CO_2 enrichment.

The two most practical methods for enriching the garden with CO_2 are a tank with a regulator and small CO_2 generators manufactured for grow spaces. Both are easy to set up and maintain.

CO2 TANKS

Large tanks hold 50 lbs. of gas, but weigh 170 lbs. filled, so they can be arduous to move around. A tank that holds 20 lbs. weighs only 50 lbs. filled and is much easier to move. To control the emission of the gas, a CO_2 tank needs a pressure regulator, a flow meter, and a solenoid valve to turn the tank on and off. The pressure regulator equalizes the pressure at which the gas flows as the tank empties. The flow meter controls the cubic feet (ft^3) of gas emitted per minute. Meters appropriate for small gardens emit between 10 and 50 cubic feet per hour. The solenoid valve turns the flow on and off.

Several kinds of switches or regulators can be used to turn the solenoid valve on or off. Some are based on timers; others are timer, and ventilation-based, replenishing the air each time outside ventilation stops.

The easiest and most accurate regulator is an on-line meter. The desired ppm is set and the meter does the rest. It requires no figuring and is the most accurate method of delivering CO_2 to the garden. It constantly measures the CO_2 level, turning the valve on or off appropriately.

With any other kind of regulator, the amount of gas to be released must be figured based on the volume of the garden. To do this, multiply the dimensions of the growing area (length × width × height).

The result is the volume of the space, which is measured in cubic feet. To find the amount of gas required to enrich the garden to 1000 ppm CO_2, multiply the cubic feet by .001; to enrich to 1500 ppm multiply by .0015 and for 2000 ppm multiply by .002. For example, a room that measures 9' × 12' × 11' totals 1188 cubic feet. Multiply this by .001 for a total of 1.18 cubic feet of gas needed to enrich the room to 1000 ppm.

For 1000 ppm, 1000 cubic feet equals 1 cubic foot of CO_2.

For 2000 ppm, 2000 cubic feet equals 1 cubic foot of CO_2.

At room temperature, there are 8.7 cubic feet in a pound of gas. To find out how much CO_2 must be injected into the air to raise the level of CO_2 to 1000 ppm, figure out the volume of the room (length × width × height). Multiply this by .001 by moving the decimal point three digits to the left. For example, a room 9' × 12' × 10' contains 1080 cubic feet. Multiplied by .001, the figure comes to 1.08 cubic feet. If the emitter is set to release two cubic feet per minute, the valve must stay on only 30 seconds. For a concentration of 1500 ppm, 45 seconds; for 2000 ppm, a full minute.

To figure out how long a gas tank will last before it is refilled, first find out how much CO_2 is used daily. For instance, a room 6' × 3' × 9' contains 162 cubic feet. The lights are on continuously and the air is enriched to 1000 ppm, or .16 cubic feet. This is done using a steady flow of 0.25 cubic feet of CO_2 per hour. Six cubic feet of gas are used per day. A 20 lb. tank holds 20 × 8.7 cubic feet, or 174 cubic feet of gas. This is divided by the daily use of 6 cubic feet for a total of 29 days of use per refill.

A simple repeating timer, which turns on the gas repetitively during the lit periods, is the most basic method of regulating delivery. Inexpensive electronic short-range timers can be programmed for eight events a day. These should be programmed for the maximum number of events starting at light on, with the last one an hour or two before lights off. A more sophisticated switch turns the gas on after the ventilation system has stopped. It quickly replenishes the area with CO_2.

The best way to enrich the garden on a timer system if there is infrequent ventilation is by injecting the air as quickly as possible. When the ventilation fan is operating all the time, and CO_2 is constantly being blown out of the garden, a small stream of CO_2 can be constantly emitted.

To find out how long the valve should stay open, divide the cubic feet of gas required by the flow rate. Multiply by 60 for the total number of minutes. If there is frequent ventilation in the room, spread out the time for enrichment by lowering the flow rate.

Once the gas moves through the valve, it should travel by tube to the garden area, where it can be released from laser tubing hung over the canopy of the plants. Laser tubing is perforated with holes every eight inches and is used for drip irrigation. It is available at garden shops.

Carbon dioxide from the tank is cooler and heavier than air, so it floats down to the tops of the plants. With good ventilation, it will mix throughout the canopy.

Carbon dioxide enrichment using a tank reduces ventilation requirements considerably for several reasons. Carbon dioxide in the air is being replenished and plants growing in a CO_2-enriched atmosphere function more efficiently at higher temperatures. Rather than trying to draw in CO_2 from the surrounding atmosphere, the aim is now to stop the gas from dispersing into it.

Small unventilated closet areas are sometimes set up with a constant flow of CO_2 enrichment when the lights are on. Well-designed, ventilated rooms are re-enriched every time the ventilation stops. Unventilated rooms, cooled with an air conditioner, need a full replenishment of CO_2 every one to two hours.

CO_2 is heavier than air and when it comes out of the tank, it is being depressurized, which makes it cold. Subsequently, the gas sinks as it enters the space. In gardens with little internal ventilation, the gas is usually dispersed using laser-drilled irrigation tubing or released in front of internal fans.

CO₂ GENERATORS

CO_2 generators burn natural gas or propane and emit CO_2, water vapor, and heat. Using a CO_2 generator in most small spaces creates a problem, since it generates a lot of heat that must be controlled, usually through ventilation. This dissipates the higher concentration of CO_2. Carbon dioxide generators are most effective in garden spaces that require heat, rather than those where excess heat must be vented. It is easier in most situations to use a tank rather than a generator. The hot CO_2 coming from generators is lighter than air and should be dispersed using a fan. Of course, anyone who works with natural or LP gas, or with fire, must be very careful.

Gardeners can use innovative approaches to supplying CO_2. Exhaust gas emitted from a stove or water heater is suitable for the garden. A garden in a room with a water heater will be enriched every time the burners are lit. Gas stoves emit CO_2, so gardens set up in kitchen areas receive additional CO_2 during cooking. Even periodic bursts of CO_2, rather than a constant supply, boost plant growth rates.

CO_2 AT A GLANCE

1. An open door or curtain is often the best solution for a small space that has a large surface-to-air ratio.

2. External ventilation blows out the used air and draws in the new. This is usually adequate for small rooms.

3. A CO_2 enrichment system consists of a tank and regulator-flow meter, and either a timer or another automatic valve. This increases the growth rate of the plants phenomenally.

4. A water heater or gas stove may supplement the garden with CO_2.

CHAPTER 10

TEMPERATURE

AIR TEMPERATURE

Temperature, humidity, and air movement all affect plant growth.

Plants' rate of metabolism, the speed at which they function and grow, is controlled by the temperature of the surrounding air.

Marijuana grows best with a temperature in the low- to mid-70°F range during the lit period, and five to ten degrees lower during the dark period. Plants grown using CO_2 have a higher metabolism and do best in a temperature in the low 80°F range during the day and in the 70°F range during the dark period.

Low temperatures, under 65°F, slow photosynthesis and growth. The difference in growth rate is not readily apparent if the temperature dips once in a while, or if the low temperatures are not extreme. However, temperatures under 50–55°F virtually stop growth. Temperatures in the 40°F range cause slight temporary tissue damage. When temperatures dip into the high 30°F range, tissue damage, which takes several days to repair, may result-especially in older plants.

Since grow spaces in basements or attics may get cool during the winter, electric or gas heaters designed for indoor use may be used to raise the temperature. Electric heaters decrease the humidity in the room as they heat the air. Gas heaters provide CO_2, moisture, and heat to the plants.

When temperatures rise above 78°F, cannabis' rate of growth slows as the plant uses part of its energy to dissipate heat and keep it supplied with water. Plants growing in CO_2-enriched air do better with temperatures ten degrees higher. The rate of growth continues to slow as the temperature rises, stopping somewhere in the 90°F range.

With the lights off, photosynthesis stops. The plant continues respiration and keeps growing, using stored sugars to fuel the process. During this period, the plant uses oxygen and emits CO_2. When the lights are turned off, the temperature in the space is likely to be lower. Plants grow well under this regimen. However, in plant growth studies, it has been observed that when plants are grown under a lower temperature during the lit rather than the unlit periods, the space between the leaves is lessened, making for a shorter, stockier plant.

ROOT TEMPERATURE

Roots are sensitive to both cool and warm temperatures. They stay healthy and thrive when they are kept in the mid-70°F range. If the room temperature is in that range, the containers and medium will also stay in that range.

Often floors are cooler than the air or the walls. Containers placed directly on a cool floor lose their heat, resulting in slower plant growth. To conserve warmth, the units can be raised above the floor using a pallet or table. They should also be insulated using a Styrofoam sheet, which is both an excellent insulation material and light reflector.

Plants can be double-potted to deal with a cold floor. Two containers the same size are fitted together. The lower pot creates an insulating air space between the medium and the floor.

Plant roots are also affected by heat. When roots get too warm, they suffer tissue damage. This is not as much of a concern with plants growing in a planting medium or in soil. Plants growing in hydroponic units are more sensitive to high temperatures. Water reservoirs in cool spaces should be fitted with aquarium heaters.

As water temperature goes up, it holds less oxygen. Warm water supplies less oxygen to the roots. This problem becomes more acute as temperatures rise, especially in stagnant water. Air pumps keep the water circulating so that more water comes in contact with the air and exchanges CO_2 for oxygen.

A growing space with both hot air and hot water can be a disaster for a garden. The effects are different in soil and hydroponics. Plants growing in soil or in a growing medium are usually less affected by fluctuations in temperature. Hydroponic units with reservoirs of water can get too hot. This affects the plants almost immediately and, if not corrected at the first signs, causes plant death.

If the roots are kept cool, the plant canopy can handle warm temperatures better. If heat is a problem, a water cooler or water chiller is the best way of bringing the temperature down. This appliance cools the water as it passes through its tubing. Water coolers are used to cool aquariums and are advertised in aquarium magazines.

Marijuana grows best when the humidity is in the range of 40% to 60%. Higher humidity creates a favorable environment for molds and fungi and interferes with the plant's ability to transpire air through the stomata (pores) found on the leaves. The pathogens affect all parts of the plant, but especially the buds, which provide a perfect environment: dark moisture-holding crevices with little air movement.

Marijuana leaves have small "hairs" covering them, which form a windbreak slowing air movement and warming the air in the microenvironment surrounding it. This air quickly loses its CO_2 and becomes saturated with water. This air must be moved away from the plant and replaced with fresh air by creating a breeze.

Increasing the rate of air change by using a fan has beneficial effects besides controlling temperature and humidity. A breeze that causes some movement of the stem increases its strength. When a plant moves in the wind, small tears develop in the tissues. The plant quickly grows new tissue, thickening the stem. A breeze also increases the amount of CO_2 available to the plant.

MAINTAINING PROPER TEMPERATURE AND HUMIDITY

No matter what kind of electric appliances are used in the garden-lights, heaters, or pumps-the energy used is eventually converted to heat. For each 100 watts of electricity, 332 British Thermal Units (BTUs) of heat are generated. A space using 1700 watts, or 1.7 kilowatts, generates 5644 BTUs. Most of this heat must be dissipated.

There are several ways to maintain the proper temperature and humidity. The easiest method is to vent the space. Small spaces, such as a closet or a shelf, are easily vented into the room because of the large portion of surface area in contact with the general space.

Normal room temperature (about 72°F) and humidity conditions (40%) are similar to those needed by the plant. Heated rooms may be a little low in humidity, but the moisture level in the microenvironment surrounding the plant is usually higher. This is caused by evaporation of water from the medium and by plant transpiration.

Open windows are not as good a solution as fans for several reasons. They present detection problems because both light and odor can escape through them. Also, plant pests living outside may be able to use a window to find new indoor feeding grounds.

SETTING UP VENTILATION

Ventilating the space to rid it of excess heat and humidity may be as simple as keeping the door open or using a central air conditioning/heating system. With small spaces, it is fairly easy to dissipate heat and moisture, since only small amounts are generated and the open space comprises a high percentage of the perimeter. Other garden spaces take up only a small part of a larger space, so there is constant air exchange.

Ventilation—that is, exchanging air—may require a fan regulated by a thermostat/humidistat. The larger the space and the more light used, the more heat and moisture are generated. These must be dissipated.

This bud is beginning to ripen. Although some stigmas are drying, it is a month away from maturity.

This bud is 20 days from harvest. The stigmas are still fresh, the ovaries are small and the glands unfilled.

This bud is 10 days from harvest. It will gain weight, glands will fill and its color will change.

This perfect bud is ready to harvest. Notice dried stigmas, enlarged ovaries and dense flowers.

Flowers can appear at the juncture of stem and leaf before forcing, as seen on this young female.

Female flowers are easily identified three weeks after forcing.

This male bud shows both immature and open flowers.

A single male flower such as this can pollinate an entire garden.

This attic garden uses closeable skylights to supplement the artificial light.

This 4x4 closet garden is lit by a 1000 watt HPS lamp.

This commercial ebb-and-flow table has been set up in an attic. The plants are growing in rockwool cubes.

These plants are growing in 32 ounce styrofoam containers on a one foot wide shelf, lit by three 8' flourescent bulbs.

This overfertilized plant is identified by the curling, dried out leaves. To save, thoroughly flush medium to remove excess nutrients.

This plant is suffering from a magnesium deficiency. The leaves have yellowed and new growth is much smaller. It can be replenished with magnesium sulfate.

This plant is wilting from lack of water. To revive, increase frequency of waterings.

The leaves on this waterlogged plant look dull and have begun to curl under. Salvage by allowing planting mix to dry out more before each watering.

This aphid has just delivered a new plant sucker. Adults are about 1/16″ long and come in many colors.

These 1/8″ plant suckers are easily seen flying off disturbed vegetation. They are vectors for disease and weaken plants.

These 1/16″ insects are detected by the trail they deposit as they bore through leaves.

These 1/32″ spotted mites are relatives of spiders. Other species come in various colors and designs.

This wick system requires attention only once a week. Supplies include: 5/8" nylon rope, kiddie pool, shipping palette and three gallon pots.

This commercial unit constantly recirculates water using a reservoir in the outer pot.

This vegetative room uses 4" rockwool cubes, each one irrigated by by a drip emitter. When plants reach 12" they are moved into a flowering room.

PLANT SUPPORTS

These plants were each trimmed to four large buds, each supported by its own stake.

Layering wide netting over the garden allows plant stems to grow through the net squares and immediately receive support.

This sativa produces a giant, but not very dense bud.

This plant will produce a compact bud in only five more weeks.

This bud is ready to be harvested. The stigmas have dried and turned red and the ovaries behind them have swelled.

It may be feasible to install a window-top ventilation fan to deal with the problem. In a smaller room, fans should have the capacity to move the room's entire volume of air every ten minutes. As an example, a fan in a 200 cubic foot grow space moves 20 cubic feet per minute.

In enclosed or larger spaces, ventilation or squirrel fans and other ventilation units mounted near the top of the wall can be used to pull out the heated air. These large spaces are subject to heat buildup so the ventilation system should be capable of moving the entire cubic volume of air out of the space every five minutes. A garden comprising most of the space in a 10' × 10' × 8' (800 cubic feet) room, should have a fan capable of moving about 150 cubic feet per minute.

Also, in larger spaces, where a lot of heat is being generated, a vent or vent fan allows fresh air to enter. If the air is coming from outside, it should be filtered through a fine mesh screen to prevent insects from gaining entrance.

In some spaces, the ventilation fans must be kept going constantly. This may make it impossible to enrich the air with CO_2. However, at the higher temperatures at which CO_2-enriched gardens are kept, the fans may be on only intermittently.

To cool the garden, the incoming air must be cooler than the garden's air. If there is not much difference between the two, the ventilation will do no good. This is not usually a problem during the winter. However, during the summer, in houses without area or central air conditioning, other cooling methods may be needed.

An air conditioner can be used to cool a space. Air conditioners exchange heat rather than air. When one is used, the space needs to be ventilated less frequently, so it is easier to maintain high CO_2 levels. The air conditioner can be built into an internal wall or installed into a curtain by being placed on a table. The unit cools the air and lowers humidity by condensing water from the air.

Humidity can be controlled using a dehumidifier hooked up to a humidistat. These remove gallons of water from the air daily, making the room much drier. The downside is that this appliance does create heat.

Grow spaces in basements or attics may get cool during the winter. An electric or gas heater (or a CO_2 generator—see Chapter 9) designed for indoor use can be used to raise the temperature. Electric heaters decrease the humidity in the room as they heat the air. Gas heaters provide CO_2, moisture, and heat to the plants.

AIR CIRCULATION

Breezes remove waste gases and humidity from the leaf's surface, replacing them with fresh air containing CO_2.

To create a breeze, so that air is exchanged at the leaf surface, fans must be used. Air movement should be forceful enough to cause a slight movement of the leaves. Ceiling, box, table fans, and uprights can all be used. Oscillating fans are often convenient. Fans with too forceful a flow can be pointed at a wall to buffer the breeze.

Closed systems deal with the entire environment by adjusting rather than exchanging the air. The air is cooled by an air conditioner. The humidity is lowered by a dehumidifier, and the CO_2 (see Chapter 9) is supplied from a tank. Each of these units is connected to a sensor so that it goes on and off automatically. The air conditioner also dehumidifies the room. A small-sized dehumidifier can keep a room at the desired humidity when the temperature is within the acceptable range.

SETTING UP THE VENTILATION

Depending on the size and configuration of the space, it may require a fan regulated by a thermostat/humidistat. The larger the space and the more light used, the more heat and moisture is generated and this must be dissipated. It may be feasible to install a window-top ventilation fan to deal with the problem.

CHAPTER 11

CONTROLLING ODOR

Minute solid particles floating in the air cause odors. Each particle has a positive electrical charge because it is missing an electron. This enables it to drift as it is drawn in changing directions by electrical attraction.

ION GENERATORS

The easiest and most effective method of eliminating odors is using electrical charges to precipitate or capture the minute particles.

Ion generators, sometimes called ion fountains, air ionizers or negative ion generators, add extra electrons to air molecules, giving them a negative charge. When such a negatively charged ion comes in contact with a positively charged dust particle, the air molecule gives up its electron. The positively charged particle is neutralized and no longer floats, since it is not influenced by electrical charges. The particle drops from the air and attaches itself to a nearby surface. It no longer produces an odor.

Ion generators are inexpensive and cost very little to operate. They usually solve odor problems in small gardens. In addition to precipitating the odor molecules, they do the same to all kinds of dust, which may include allergens, molds, and fungi.

Ion generators are small and use very little electricity. They can be kept in the garden, where they eliminate the odor, but not the potency of the developing buds. For the buds to develop an odor, the units should be placed outside the growing space, in the areas surrounding it, during the last three weeks of flowering. This eliminates the odors as they leave the grow space, but allows the buds themselves to develop their fragrance.

The electrical charge of the air also influences behavior and plant growth. Negatively charged air promotes a sense of well-being, as opposed to positively charged air that promotes discomfort and irritability. Negative ions are generated in nature by waves and waterfalls. Dry winds, such as the Santa Ana, carry positive ions.

OZONE GENERATORS

As a gas, oxygen (O) floats in the air as a molecule composed of two O atoms, O_2. Ozone generators produce an unstable form of O, O_3, known as ozone. When ozone comes in contact with odor molecules and dust particles, it oxidizes them, eliminating them as odor producers.

Ozone generators are more effective than negative ions in eliminating odor problems in large gardens. Health problems are not associated with the levels of ozone generated by these units. Ozone generators are more expensive than negative ion generators and should be considered only when the ion units are not totally effective.

ELECTROSTATIC PRECIPITATORS

These units are usually placed in central heating, air conditioning units, and exhaust flues. They create an electrical charge over a filter of wires. When air flows through the filter, solid particles are captured, eliminating odor. When these units can be fitted into furnaces, they are very helpful in eliminating odor and dust.

AIR CLEANERS

Housewares stores sell air cleaners that circulate air using several filters and negative ions to capture dust and odor. High-quality models are very effective in dealing with odor problems. These units are designed to harmonize with living spaces.

CHAPTER 12

PREPARING THE SPACE

Once the space is chosen, it must be prepared for the garden. Electricity, reflective material and floors must all be installed and cleaned.

CLEANLINESS

By gardening in a clean area with no unneeded objects around, there is less chance of accidents and spills, it is easier to work and there is less chance of infecting the plants.

First, all extraneous material should be removed from the space, or at least placed in boxes or thoroughly covered. Next, the space should be thoroughly vacuumed. If there are any spaces or holes in the walls that connect to the outside they should be sealed so to prevent air or light from passing through. This also stops insects and other plant pests from entering and leaves no room for suspicion by anyone outside.

It may be possible to make these seals with several layers of duct tape or they may need plastering or woodworking. Windows should also be sealed so that no suspicious light reaches the outside. A piece of cardboard or plywood or a few layers of 6-mil black polyethylene will accomplish this. To avoid the suspicious look of a blacked out window, curtains, drapes or venetian blinds may be placed so they face the outside.

Once the room is orderly and vacuumed, it is time to wash-down using a household cleaner such as ammonia, 409® or Citrus-Solve® so that the room becomes more hygienic.

ELECTRICITY

For their size, indoor marijuana gardens are large electricity drains. The lit space of a garden typically uses between 20 and 60 watts per square foot, and other appliances such as air conditioners, pumps, fans, water heaters and light movers increase the load.

It is extremely important that the wiring is adequate to support the electrical draw. If the wiring is inadequate, shorts, resulting in unanticipated power failures are likely. Even more serious, a fire can occur.

Electrical matters must be taken care of before the garden is started. It is very impractical to make improvements after the grow has begun.

The wiring should be more than adequate to carry the load. The load is the total watts that will be consumed at peak use. The light is the biggest electric user, with ratings of 250-, 400- or 1000-watts per lamp. The other appliances state their wattage, too. The total wattage should be increased by 40% when wiring is designed to make sure that the lines have plenty of reserve capacity.

The garden's electrical requirements have been figured in watts, but the appliances are rated in amps. To convert watts to amps divide the total wattage by 120, the rated voltage in North America (W/V=A). For instance, one 25 square foot garden lit by a 1000 watt lamp, and using fans, air conditioner, water heater, pumps and meters has a total peak need of 2000 watts. It is unlikely that the current will ever be used at that rate, but if all the appliances were running at the same time it would reach this peak. Multiply the 2000 by 140% for a total of 2800 watts. The extra 40% accounts for hidden wattage such as ballasts and line resistance and provides a reserve so the wires are never electrically challenged. Divided by 120 (the voltage). The total capacity required for the garden is 23 amps.

Each circuit in both houses and apartments has either a circuit breaker or a fuse. The electrical rating of the circuit can be found at this junction.

One circuit is usually enough to meet a small garden's needs, but a space may need to import electricity from more than one circuit. This is best done using electrical tubing or conduit by someone who knows how to do it.

Whether electricity is imported from another space or is tapped from a wall outlet, working electrical outlets should be placed well above the floor at a convenient level to work at while standing, so plugs can easily be pulled and the lines are above the water line. No electrical cords should lie on the floor. Instead, wiring should be placed high along the walls or hang down from the ceiling. This minimizes the likelihood of water touching them.

Small spaces may require only one area to plug in to, but large spaces may require more outlets placed in several spots to eliminate the need for extension cords and hanging wires. If extension cords are used, they should be adequate for the current they carry and should have three lines (three prong plug) for grounded appliances.

Grounded appliances should always be plugged into grounded, three line receptacles. If these are unavailable, the third line (the grounding line) should be attached to an electrical ground such as metal plumbing. This too should be done by someone familiar with wiring. A good explanation for having this work done is that the outlet is to be used for electronic equipment, such as a computer.

Electronic equipment, such as meters, should be connected through surge protectors. These units usually must be connected to a grounded outlet to function properly.

FLOORS

Floors not made for spills and wetness should be protected. Carpets, linoleum and wood floors should be covered with a liner so that water cannot get to these surfaces. This is extremely important because it prevents damage in case of an accident or even a small spill.

Anywhere there is water there is a chance of spills and accidents. Although accidents happen, if the space is well-designed, a spill will be easy to deal with.

Rubber pool lining is especially made to hold water and the best material that can be used. Waterproof plastic tarps and polyethylene can also be used.

A heavy layer of newspaper under the liner will absorb moisture should the liner develop any small holes, which is highly unlikely. For even more security, a newspaper sandwich can be installed. First a liner is laid on the floor. Then a layer of newspaper, followed by a liner on top of the paper.

VENTILATION

Most small systems only need a fan to exchange air with the space outside the grow room. If the growing space needs an elaborate ventilation system, it should be installed by a knowledgeable craftsperson.

FINAL INSTALLATIONS

The space has been prepared. The floors are protected, the wall is lined with reflective material, the electrical system and the outlets are plug in ready and the ventilation has been installed. The next step is to set up the garden.

First timers and controllers should be securely attached and plugged in. Then they should be set.

Hanging the lighting can be as simple as screwing a U hook in the ceiling. Light movers may be attached directly to the ceiling. However they are sometimes attached to a board in a way that they can easily be removed, such as with wing bolts. The board is then securely attached to the ceiling with mollies or other appropriate fasteners. The light should be hooked up to the light timer.

Internal fans should be installed. They can be hung from the ceiling, or placed on a table or shelf. A floor fan may be a convenient alternative. The outside ventilation fan should be hooked up to a thermostat/humidistat.

The air conditioner, if being used, should be plugged into the thermostat/humidistat, which is installed in the grow room.

The CO_2 unit should be hooked up and turned on. If it is being regulated by a meter, the meter should be placed at canopy level so there is an accurate reading of CO_2 ppm at plant level.

Everything is ready except for the containers or hydroponic unit. Now is the time to install the system, including trays, reservoirs, containers and anything else the system requires.

PREPARING THE MIX

Once everything else is set up, it is time to get the growing unit installed. The hydroponic units or trays for planting medium have been set up. It is time to fill the hydroponic unit reservoir with water, prepare the mix and run the system to make sure that the timers and everything else in the garden is working.

The first consideration in preparing mixes is always safety. Many of the ingredients create dust when they are moved around. Some of the dusts such as from vermiculite and perlite are carcinogenic. Dusts from the other ingredients are not healthy to breathe, either.

To prevent problems, the ingredients should be moistened to eliminate dust before use, as mentioned earlier. This can be accomplished by opening the package and wetting the mix with a sprinkling can. The water should contain a wetting agent to break surface tension. A teaspoon of dishwashing liquid per gallon of water works well for this.

Dry vermiculite and perlite are very prone to dust. If they are not wetted down the mixer should work in an area with good ventilation, wear rubber or garden gloves and long sleeved clothing, and use a respirator. However, the best way to deal with this is to prevent the dust in the first place by pre-wetting the medium.

It is easier to get the ingredients mixed consistently when the medium is prepared in small batches. The ingredients can be mixed more thoroughly, and reasonable size mixing containers can be used.

A large plastic or small galvanized tub is an excellent container for preparing mixes and filling pots. When vermiculite or perlite or any other dusty medium is used, take either a hose or watering can and thoroughly wet the medium. The water soaks through about six inches of a three-and-one-half cubic foot bag. When the moistened level fades to dry, it is time to water the medium again. With moistened ingredients there is no dust, so the pot can be stirred with rubber gloved hands. Six to eight 6" pots-worth of ingredients is a comfortable amount to mix at a time.

BEFORE BEGINNING

Before a seed is planted or a cutting transferred to the new garden, successful growers make sure the space is ready. Here is a general checklist and the order in which the garden is generally constructed.

1. **Electricity**—Make sure there is adequate electricity available to safely power the garden. This is not usually a problem in small gardens but in larger gardens, this may entail bringing in power from several circuits. Place all ballasts and other equipment, outlets, extension cords, switches and timers off the floor and away from water. Check to make sure all lighting and electrical equipment is working.

2. **Ventilation or cooling system**—Install the ventilation or cooling system. Check that the space stays in the correct temperature range for several cycles.

3. **Hydroponic system**—Make sure that it is working properly.

4. **Soil Based System**—The containers should be ready for seeds or cuttings.

5. **Reflective material**—This is essential because plant growth is based on light. A grower should check that the reflective material is in place and securely fastened.

6. **CO2**—Check to make sure that the regulator is working properly.

No matter what kind of system is being used, successful growers try a final test run. They make sure that lights, water delivery, drainage, CO_2, ventilation, and everything else in the space is ready. Pumps and timers are carefully inspected to make sure they are working properly. It is much easier to repair the system before plants are growing in it.

CHAPTER 13

SEEDS OR CLONES

There are two ways to start a garden; from seed or from clones. There are some advantages to starting with seeds. However, it is usually easier to start and maintain a garden using clones. If you are lucky enough to be able to start with clones from excellent indoor varieties suited to your garden type, that is the way to go. Clones are much easier and make much more sense.

CLONE ADVANTAGES

Nearly everyone has taken a cutting from a houseplant and placed it in water. Within a short time, roots grew and the new plant was placed in a container with planting medium. The new plant's growth, flowers and reactions to environment were exactly the same as the plant from which it was taken. With clones the genetic make-up, and therefore the characteristics of a plant, are known. The characteristics of plants started from seed cannot be determined until the plant matures.

Plant lineage provides some information, but there is no way of determining a seed's exact qualities, or even its sex. There are literally billions of possible combinations of genes that the two parents can supply. No two plants from seed are likely to be identical, especially since many of the new "varieties" are crosses of unstabilized hybrids. The result is that with many of the commercial hybrid seeds, each of the ten seeds from a pack is likely to have an individual look, rather than the group having uniformity.

The advantages of growing genetically identical plants are:

1. Cuttings to make clones are usually taken from genetically superior female plants. This cuts out the guess-work when looking for a superior plant. It also gets a new crop going quickly without a long start-up time.

2. There will be no males in the garden. This saves valuable garden space and eliminates worry about unwanted pollination.

3. Clones grow with shorter internode length (distance between leaves on the stem) which results in shorter, stouter plants.

4. It is easy to get variety in a clone garden by growing several varieties.

5. Clones from the same plant have uniform growth characteristics so the garden is easier to maintain. Each variety's growth habits are established. In a uniform garden each plant grows to the same size. If the garden contains several varieties, each plant's needs can be accommodated.

SEEDS

Seeds may be the most convenient way to start a garden. Many gardeners do not have access to clones. Seeds are usually more readily available.

Seeds offer a way of starting a garden which is definitely free of infections. There is no way of knowing what diseases, pests or pesticides a clone from someone else's garden has.

Each seed is a genetic blueprint of an individual plant. Most commercial marijuana "varieties" exhibit quite a bit of variation. So a group of seeds may contain a real winner.

Seeds allow for genetic progression. In a clone garden, no breeding can take place so the genetic line remains static. There are no surprises and no new finds. With seeds, breeding can occur, leading to genetic surprises and new discoveries.

GERMINATING SEEDS

To germinate, marijuana seeds require moisture which seeps through the seed coat and signals the seed to start the process. The seed should be kept moist. It germinates fastest when the temperature is kept in the 70° range. Once the seed germinates it requires light and nutrients.

When the medium is cool, germination slows and the seeds may be attacked by fungi and molds. Growing in high temperatures, seedlings grow thin and spindly, especially under low light conditions. Under low light conditions, plants, especially seedlings, stretch. The stem elongates and is very thin.

PLANTING METHODS

There are two ways of planting seeds. They can be started between wet napkins or a cloth that is kept constantly moist. Adding a teaspoon of bleach per cup of water prevents pathogens from attacking the seeds. A dilute bloom fertilizer solution aids germination. As soon as the seeds show signs of germination they are placed in the medium.

It is important not to wait to plant until the root starts elongating. Improper handling or delays in planting the germinated seed can hurt the seedling. Once the seed starts germinating it grows very quickly; the difference between successful germination and marijuana sprouts is less than 24 hours.

Once the root makes an appearance, the germinating seed is placed in a quarter inch of planting medium or in the hydroponic unit as directed. The medium is placed in the container and thoroughly watered until runoff appears. A hole one-quarter to one-half inch deep is poked into the medium and the slightly germinated seed is dropped into it.

It is easier for the seeds when they are planted directly in the medium in which they are to grow. They can be placed directly into the hole. The direction that the seed faces is not important. The seed will direct its' roots downward and the stem upward.

Marijuana can be planted in a two-inch pot or block. The advantage to starting small is that the plants do not take up unused space. Seedlings are transplanted using the same techniques described under cuttings.

Rockwool and Oasis® cubes are often used for seed germination. The one-and-one-half-inch cube will support a six-inch plant as long as it is watered and fertilized regularly. They are easy and convenient to use and can be moved into any system, planting medium or hydroponic. The seed is dropped down the pre-drilled hole in the cube and left uncovered. Rockwool should be soaked in a high acidity (pH of 5.5, see Chapter 14, "Nutrients, Fertilizers and pH.") water solution for a day before being used. This neutralizes its naturally high alkalinity. Rockwool contains no nutrients and Oasis® cubes only a dilute 1-1-1 fertilizer, which helps germination.

LIGHT

Once the seedling breaks ground and comes in contact with light, it starts to photosynthesize, thus producing its own food for growth. When the light is dim, the plant stretches to reach it. In the wild, the seedling is in competition for canopy space with all the other seedling. By growing taller it may be able to reach unobstructed light. However, a stretched seedling is weaker than one with a shorter but thicker stem and have a tendency to fall over. Seedlings with ample light grow squat, thick stems.

Seedlings should be grown in constant bright light. They can be grown under MH lamps (see Chapter 8). The light should not be as intense as it will be later so 400-watt lamps should be kept about three feet above the tops and 1000-watt lamps four feet. Over a period of ten days the light should be lowered eighteen inches to deliver a more intense light. HPS lamps may induce minor flowering and a bit of stretching in some varieties.

Fluorescents can also be used for seedlings. Cool white lamps and Chroma 5000® promote vigorous growth and stocky stems. They discourage side branching in some varieties. The plants won't grow as quickly under this regimen, but they will be very high quality. For each foot of width, two to three tubes should be used. They should initially be positioned about one foot above the plants and lowered to about six inches.

Once the seedlings appear they should be irrigated with water-nutrient solution described in Chapter 14, "Nutrients, Fertilizers and pH."

HOW TO MAKE CLONES

Clones can be made from both green tissue and the woody section cuttings. Both root fairly easily. The cut is made with a very sharp sterile razor blade, knife or high quality scissors. All make clean straight cuts.

A blade may be sterilized by dipping it in alcohol or a bleach solution of one teaspoon per cup. As groups of cuttings are made, they are placed cuts stem down in a jar containing lukewarm water so they do not become dehydrated.

The cuttings are trimmed of all leaves and branches except for the top three pairs and the growing tip. All branching at the leaf joint should be removed. If the leaves and branches were left on, they would create water demands that the stem without roots cannot meet. The stem should be cut between two and five inches.

After trimming, the cut is dipped in a rooting solution such as Woods™, Hormex® or other brand, then placed in a Rockwool or Oasis® cube, a rooting medium such as vermiculite or perlite used in trays or two inch pots, or oxygenated water.

Making a Clone

First the stems are cut from the branch. Next the larger leaves are trimmed off, resulting in a bare stem with leaves only at the top. Then they are gathered, lining up the tops of the leaves, and the stems are trimmed evenly.

The ends are then dipped into a rooting solution. Finally, they are placed into 1.5"×1.5" rockwool cubes in a 10"×20" tray.

The cuttings are placed in a tray and covered with a transparent cover to retain the moisture. The cover is kept on the tray for about five days and then removed. The trays are placed under ten to fifteen watts of light from a fluorescent Cool White, Chroma SPX 50, or the equivalent placed about one to two feet above the top of the tray. They can be kept under constant light or a cycle of eighteen hours on, six hours off. The trays are watered every other day with a mix of vegetative and flowering formula diluted to about 400 ppm. Water can remain in the tray to provide moisture, but should not touch the roots.

The clones should be kept at 72°F to 75°F. A horticultural heating mat or heating cable can be placed under the tray to maintain warmth if the space is too cool. Higher and lower temperatures delay rooting and increase the failure rate.

Within seven to ten days roots should appear. At the same time, new growth appears on the plant tops. The fertilizer should be changed to vegetative formula at about 800 ppm. As soon as the clone begins vigorous growth it is ready to go into the garden. Some varieties are easier to root than others, so success rates vary.

PLANTING SEEDS AND CLONES

Both seeds and clones are easy to plant and are ready to grow rapidly.

If the plant was grown in a Rockwool or Oasis® cube it is ready to plant when its roots extend from the medium or block. Grown in a container with medium, it should have enough of a root system to form a rootball, a root system large enough to hold the medium. Topside, it should have three to four sets of well developed leaves, or for clones, several new pairs of leaves.

Only the best-looking plants should be chosen to transplant. Clones should look vigorous, with no deformities on the leaves. The top should form a rosette and the growing tip should be green.

Male seedlings will have to be removed from the space, so seedlings should be placed in the garden at twice the density at which

Potting a Seedling or Clone

This seedling's roots have pushed their way outside the cube it's been rooting in; an indication it's ready for potting. The cube is then planted in a 6" deep pot to allow the roots to spread out and the plant to grow. After the cube is fully covered, the dirt is tamped down with gloved hands.

they are to finish. Male plants have a tendency to grow faster than females during initial growth stages. The plants with the best development should be chosen, not necessarily the tallest.

When a commercial hydroponic system is being used, their directions should be followed. In planting medium or container systems the unit should be filled to the level the rootball or cube will be placed. The plant is put inside and the unit is filled to one inch below the top. If the distance between the root system and the bottom leaf is more than three inches, the stem should be buried so that only three inches is above the soil line.

In shallow trays the rootball should be buried below the soil line, but on Rockwool or P.U. slabs the cube is placed directly on top of the slab and the roots grow right into it.

CHAPTER 14

NUTRIENTS, FERTILIZERS AND pH

Plants require nutrients in order to grow. The roots absorb the nutrients from the water as dissolved salts. These are the simple compounds found in chemical fertilizers. Organic fertilizers travel a more circuitous route, first breaking down from complex molecules through microbial action, and then dissolving into the water.

Nitrogen (N), phosphorus (P), and potassium (K) are called the macronutrients because plants use large quantities of them. The percentages of N, P, and K ar always listed in the same order (N-P-K) on fertilizer packages.

Calcium (Ca), sulfur (S), and magnesium (Mg) are also required in fairly large quantities. They are often called secondary nutrients.

Smaller amounts of iron (Fe), zinc (Zn) manganese (Mn) boron (B), cobalt (Co), copper (Cu), molybdenum (Mo), and chlorine (Cl) are also required. These are called micronutrients.

Plants that are being grown in soil mixes or mixes with nutrients added, such as compost, worm castings, or manure, do better when watered with a dilute soluble fertilizer too. When a non-nutritive medium, or hydroponics, is being used, the nutrients are supplied as a solution in the water from the beginning.

If the garden has been set up for hydroponics, it is best to use a complete hydroponic formula. These are especially formulated to be water-soluble and provide all the plant's nutrient needs. Some of them are also pH balanced, which is a measure of the alkaline-acid ratio.

High-tech garden shops sell a number of different brands. Each brand has its adherents, who claim it is the only one to use. Each has a different formula, making the choice bewildering.

Typical formulas for the seedlings and early-growth stage, the first ten days, include 7-9-5, 18-18-21, and 4-5-3. However, it is common practice to skip these and use vegetative growth formulas during seedling and clone stages. High P formulas promote thicker stems and accentuated root growth, but they obviously are not necessary.

Once the plants are past the clone or seedling stage and have begun rapid growth, they should receive a growth formula. Many growers use high priced fertilizers, but I haven't seen any real difference in growth between them and other complete formulas which are soluble, such as Miracle Gro® 18-18-21 or Peter's® 20-20-20.

Formulas for the fastest growth stage usually have a little more N than other nutrients. However, in a warm garden this is not necessary. Plants growing under warm conditions (over 80°F) are given less N to prevent stem etiolation. Plants grown in cool environments are given more N.

During flowering, a high P formula promotes flower growth. Fertilizers with ratios such as 5-20-10, 2-4-3, 3-20-20 and 2-10-10 are also used.

Some hydroponic formulas, especially two or three part mixes increase K along with P. The problem is that P is very acidic and upsets the pH balance. One solution that fertilizer manufacturers use is to balance the acidic P with alkaline K, even though non-fruiting flowering plants don't use much of it.

Plants are sometimes grown using a nutrient solution containing no N for the last ten days. Many of the larger leaves will turn yellow and wither as N migrates from old to new growth.

Fertilizer should be complete; that is, it should contain all the secondary and trace elements. Fertilizers list all of their ingredients. If secondary nutrients are not listed, then they are not in the mix.

Sometimes growers prefer to use more than one fertilizer. In this case, each fertilizer should be added directly to the reservoir. Fertilizers should not be mixed together.

Over-fertilization is very dangerous. When plants are under-fertilized, more nutrients can be added. Over-fertilization can quickly kill a plant. Growers should be careful never to add more fertilizer than is recommended.

Growers take no chances by changing hydroponic nutrient-water solutions every two weeks. Even though the solution may have nutrients left, it is probably unbalanced, since the plants have used some of the nutrients and not others.

The water being used can affect plant growth and fertilization. Water with high salt levels (over 200 ppm dissolved solids) can cause nutrient imbalances. In that case, water can be filtered or mixed with low ppm water, reverse osmosis or steam distillation are suitable filtering processes to remove unwanted salts.

Some fertilizers are complete except for magnesium (Mg). This is easily supplemented with Epsom salts ($MgSO_4$) at one-quarter teaspoon per gallon of water (one teaspoon for four gallons, or one tablespoon for twelve gallons). Epsom salts are readily available at most drugstores.

Other fertilizers lack calcium (CA), this can be supplied using liquid calcium, liquid bone meal or calcium nitrate. Although you can follow directions on the label of the fertilizers and commercial hydroponic units as to watering, the only way to really get a handle on the situation is to be able to measure the concentration of the fertilizer in the water. This is most easily done using an EC (electrical conductivity) meter, which will give a rough approximation of the ppm of the dissolved solids-that is, the combination of the minerals in the tap water and the fertilizer.

Tap water with a ppm lower than 100 is ideal, water with a ppm of over 200 is problematical and should be filtered to bring down the level of dissolved solids.

Hydroponic systems usually have water nutrient solutions of 900–1600 ppm although some growers use higher or lower concentrations with very successful results. In part, it depends on the variety, since some have idiosyncratic fertilizer requirements. With a water nutrient solution in the 1000–1300ppm range the plants in most gardens are sure to have enough nutrients for vigorous growth. A space that is lit especially brightly should use higher concentrations of nutrient.

NUTRIENT PROBLEMS

Slight, chronic over-fertilizing can cause the leaves to curl either upward or underneath and brown at the tip. Heavy over-fertilizing can cause the plant to wilt in a matter of minutes. When the soil medium has a higher concentration of salts (nutrients) than the plant, it draws water from the plant. The only solution to this problem is to get rid of the excess nutrient by rinsing it out. Once the plant starts to wilt, a few minutes may mean life or death.

SYMPTOMS AND TREATMENT

The nutrient deficiencies that a plant is most likely to encounter are iron (Fe), magnesium (Mg) nitrogen (N), phosphorous (P), potassium (K) and zinc (Zn). The symptoms and treatments for these deficiencies are given below.

- **Fe**—Pale or white growing shoots leaving only the veins green. It affects only the new growth. Iron-zinc-manganese liquid should be sprayed on the plant for immediate relief, which should appear in a few days. This supplement should be added to the water, as well.

- **Mg**—First the lower leaves turn yellow, leaving only the veins green. The tips of the lower leaves curl upward and die. Then the new growth turns white, leaving only the veins green. The plants should be sprayed with a solution of one teaspoon Epsom salts per quart of water. If the fertilizer has Mg listed as an ingredient, one-quarter teaspoon per gallon of water should be added, one-half teaspoon if not. The plants should respond within a few days.

- **N**—Lower leaves turn pale green, then yellow, then die as the N travels to new growth, and stems and leaf stems turn purple. These plants should be watered with a high N liquid fertilizer.

- **P**—Plants have small dark green leaves and red veins. Tips of lower leaves die. Then the entire leaves yellow and die. During bloom plants need large amounts of P to develop large flowers. Low levels result in small flowers. These plants should be watered with a high P liquid fertilizer.

- **K**—Slight deficiences result in tall plants with thinner stems. Larger deficiencies are most apparent on the large leaves (sun leaves) in the middle of the plant. They develop necrotic patches and turn pale green. The stems and leaf stems may turn deep red or purple. These plants will respond to fertilization with a high K liquid fertilizer.

- **Zn**—New growth looks twisted and curled and does not develop. Plants in this condition should be sprayed with an iron-zinc-manganese (I-Zn-Mn) liquid fertilizer, and it should also be added to the water-nutrient mix.

PH

The measure of acid-alkalinity balance of a solution is called the pH of a solution. It is measured on a scale of 1–14 with 1 being the most acidic, 7 is neutral, and 14 is most alkaline. Nutrients are most soluble in a limited range of acidity from about 5.8–6.8. Various nutrients fall out of solution on the edges of that range. Although the mineral may be present, it is not available to the plant.

When nutrients are locked up, plants cannot grow. Typically, a plant growing in an environment with pH levels that are too high or low is very small, often growing only a few inches in several months. Plants growing in a high pH environment look pale and sickly and also have stunted growth. If the water or soil is kept near a pH of 6.5 all of the nutrients the plant needs will be readily soluble and available to the plants.

The acidity/alkalinity of a solution is measured using aquarium or garden pH chemical test kits, pH paper or a pH meter. All are accurate and easy to use. The pH should be tested after fertilizers have been added to the water.

In both medium and hydroponic systems the best way to solve the problem of unbalanced pH is by adjusting the water-nutrient solution with either pH Up or Down, available at high tech grow stores. Sulphuric acid or phosphoric acid are the usual ingredients in pH Down. In medium based systems, sulphur is added to bring the pH Down. The main ingredient of pH Up is hydrogen.

Growers sometimes use baking soda to raise the pH, but this is very inefficient. In planting mediums, hydrated lime is used to raise pH.

Plants affect the pH of the water solution as they remove various nutrients. Microbes growing in the medium also change the pH. Whenever the water is changed or added the pH should be checked and adjusted. In addition, the water should be checked and pH adjusted every few days.

CHAPTER 15

CARE DURING VEGETATIVE GROWTH

Once the seeds have sprouted, the plants begin a period of fast stem and leaf growth. This is known as the vegetative growth stage. With good conditions, plants grow from three to four sets of leaves within the first ten days. After that, they really take off, growing both top and side branches. By the end of the first month, a stocky plant usually grows to between one and one-and-one-half feet. After two months of growth, plants grow to between two and three feet, depending on conditions and variety. Plants grown using intense light and CO_2 grow faster.

Clones in an adequate sized container grow very quickly, usually faster than seedlings for the first few weeks. Clones develop a stockier stem, with shorter internodes, and their branching patterns may also be different than their sisters grown from seed.

LIGHT

During vegetative growth, the plants do best when the lights are kept on continuously. The plants do not need a "rest period." Some growers cut the expense of running high-watt lamps 24 hours a day by turning them off for one to six hours. However, costs other than light, such as rent, labor, and risk remain fixed no matter how the light cycle is set.

The garden is at maximum efficiency on a continuous light cycle. It actually costs growers more to grow an ounce of bud using an 18-hour cycle rather than a continuous one Of course, meter considerations may dictate a break in the light period.

IRRIGATION

Reservoir and wick hydroponic systems are self-regulating; the medium draws water from the reservoir to maintain an even level of moisture. The reservoirs must be refilled periodically. Large plants use more water than small ones, so their reservoirs must be checked more often. Once the reservoir is filled with nutrient-water mix, any water added should be pH-adjusted and should be maintained nutrient-free.

Active hydroponic systems have different schedules of irrigation. Drip systems with moist mediums such as vermiculite, perlite, or rockwool are usually watered one to four times a day. Systems using dry mediums such as hydrostone or gravel are often on drip or flow constantly but a minimum of four times a day.

Ebb-and-flow systems with moist mediums are irrigated once every day or two. Dry mediums are irrigated two to four times a day.

For all hydroponic systems water should be changed twice each month. Water added between changes should be pH adjusted and nutrient free.

Plants growing in planting medium must also be kept moist. Generally they should be watered when the top (one inch) layer of medium feels dry. Even if the garden is not scheduled to be watered, if the medium feels dry, it should be watered.

The containers should never be allowed to get so dry that the plants wilt. Here are some generalities about watering.

• If the plants are small and the garden is in a cool space, it should be watered every four or five days.

• If the plants are large, but in small containers, and the garden is in a warm space, the garden may need to be watered daily.

- The containers should be irrigated until they drain.

- Lukewarm water (in the low 70°F range) should be used, to avoid shocking or burning the roots.

NUTRIENTS

Fertilizers are best used as directed. The worst thing a garener can do is over-fertilize, since this can cause sudden death in plants. The nutrient water solution is changed twice monthly. The old water is drained and replaced with a fresh nutrient-water solution. The system does not have to be rinsed. The old water is suitable for use in the outdoor garden.

PRUNING

Not only do plants of different varieties grow to different heights, but their branching patterns are different. Some have rather short branches, so that most of the main budding occurs along the main stem. Others have long branches which attempt to get a piece of the canopy. No matter how big the plants will be allowed to get, the number of branches, or leads, should be limited on each plant.

Plants growing four-per-square-foot or denser should have only one main stem. Plants growing in larger areas, one-per-square-foot, may have up to five or six leads. A plant growing in three square feet may have ten or more.

To limit the number of leads, the plants should be pruned. This should be done in a consistent way so that all the plants get their share of the canopy. Once the desired number of leads is established, new branches are removed using pruning shears or scissors.

If there are several varieties growing in the same garden some are probably taller than others. This can be a problem. There are two ways of solving it. One is to prune the plant. If the top is cut off, the plant will then put its energy into the branches surrounding the center growth. The other way is to crease a branch. The branch is bent until some of the tissue snaps. The branch will quickly grow new tissue to

Pruning to Leads

These plants have been pruned to 2, 3, 4, and 6 leads, respectively. Note that each lead is given its own stake.

This technique maximizes top quality, large, potent buds rather than a lot of small, lesser quality buds from lower branches.

repair the damage, but the snapped part lets the plant develop buds all along the now-horizontal central stem.

SUPPORTS

With the ideal conditions that indoor gardens can supply plants, they need help supporting the prodigious buds that they grow. There are a number of ways to provide it. The simplest is using stakes which are placed in the soil or medium and to which plants are tied using twist-ties. By keeping the branches and buds upright, and not arching over or into others, each plant gets its share of the light.

Another way of supporting the plants is to build an overhead frame and tie the plants to it.

CHAPTER 16

FLOWERING

The goal of the closet cultivator is to grow plants which yield a large crop of sinsemilla, the unfertilized female flowers of the plant. Usually male and female flowers grow on separate plants. By removing the male plants from the garden, the females remain unpollinated. Pollinated plants put most of their energy into producing seeds, rather than bud growth.

Unpollinated plants grow clusters of flowers over a period of six to ten weeks. Within a few weeks of forcing, the growth takes the shape of a bud. As the buds ripen, the clusters of flowers grow thicker and the resin glands found on the small leaves and branches begin to swell as they fill up with THC. As the bud ripens it begins to fluoresce.

WHEN TO FLOWER

Indoors, marijuana can be forced to flower at any time. Even seedlings indicate sex and produce flowers under forcing conditions. The decision of when to flower should be based on two factors: the amount of space each plant has, and the variety's growth habits.

Marijuana flowers in response to the light cycle. Outdoors, it is a fall-flowering plant. The plant senses the oncoming autumn by chemically measuring the length of the uninterrupted dark period. Indoors, when the light regimen includes a dark period of 12 hours during each 24 hour period, the plant switches from vegetative growth to reproductive mode. It grows male or female flowers, which usually occur on separate plants. As long as this light regimen is maintained, the plant will continue to grow flowers.

The importance of this is that flowering is not based on the plant's chronological age or size, just on the lighting regimen it receives. Marijuana plants can be forced to flower at any size, even when they are quite small. By regulating the light cycle you determine the size of the plant at maturity.

When light hits a leaf, the tissue absorbs certain rays which it uses in photosynthesis. Those rays are unavailable to leaves below the top. 1000-watt HID lamps penetrate only the first twelve to eighteen inches of leaves, depending on their size and quantity. Vegetative material below this canopy receives little light, does little photosynthesizing and produces little energy for the plant.

Since a tall plant produces no larger yield than a short one, the plants are forced to flower when they are eight to 15 inches tall. At maturity they will stand only 18 to 36 inches in height.

PRUNING

The size desired for the finished plant determines the pruning techniques used in the garden. Plants which are left unpruned as they go into flowering have many small buds and dense undeveloped undergrowth, rather than a bigger yield from fewer, larger buds.

There are many pruning techniques. Some were described in Chapter 15. About two weeks into flowering, or in some instances, as the plants are forced, the plants should be pruned.

Extraneous branches and fan leaves which block light to the buds are removed using scissors or clippers. Usually the branches and leaves are cut off at the base, where they meet the stem. However, they can be cut in other ways.

For instance, the Bob Marley strains, which are partly Jamaican, have long branches coming off a main stem. These branches have long internodes so they stretch into other plants' areas. The solution is to cut the branches so they stay within the plant's area. By the second or third week of flowering, the plant is unlikely to start new branch growth, but will put its energy into bud growth.

Leaves that are blocking light to buds should be removed or pruned. This light promotes growth in the newly lit buds. The tips or fingers of the leaves sometimes stretch beyond their allotted space. They can be trimmed using scissors so that they don't infringe on other plants' space.

When single-stem plants are placed in flowering all growing tips which occur at the node where the leaf and the stem meet, should be removed. At the canopy only one main stem should be left. Plants which are growing on larger centers can support four, six, or even eight branches, depending on the area the plant has to grow in. Each bud-holding branch requires a circle of between four and eight inches.

Even if the plant wasn't pruned during vegetative growth, or especially if it wasn't, it should pruned down, leaving only the branches holding large buds near the canopy. The smaller lower branches, even the tiny ones, should be removed. Then, depending on the plant's shape, leave only the branches that have access to the canopy. The number of leads a plant should have depends on the size of the desired ripe plant.

MALE FLOWERS

With cuttings, there will be no male plants, but plants from seeds the males have to be removed. To do this, the lights are switched to short cycle: 12 hours on, 12 hours off. When the flowers appear, a photographer's loupe or a magnifying glass is used to identify the male flowers.

Males usually indicate first. The unripe flowers look like small pawnbrokers' balls hanging from the stem, or a small cluster of grapes. The mature flowers have five very small white or yellow petals and a lot of pollen. As soon as any male plants indicate sex, before the flowers open, they should be removed from the garden. This prevents the females from being pollinated.

The immature female flowers are oval, pointed up, and have a very thin hair-like stigma.

Here are the stages of flower growth:

1. Slowdown, then stop of vegetative growth. Four to ten days after beginning of forcing. Lasts up to a week.

2. Appearance of first flowers. Ten to fifteen days after beginning of forcing.

3. Massive growth of flowers at the budding sites, continuing after the first appearance of flowers for 30 to 40 days. During this time, the buds develop and take shape. Starting with a few flowers, layer after layer of flowers is grown until the bud sides are merged together into one large cola.

4. Maturation is reached when the stigmas start to turn color from pale white to red or brown. At the same time, ripening, ovaries behind each flower begin to swell, forming false seed pods. The small glands on the flowers swell. These are called stalked capitate glands and are composed of a tiny stalk supporting a thin clear membrane.

As THC is produced near the site, the membrane fills with the potent liquid. The membrane stretches and the gland takes on the appearance of a mushroom. When the glands have swelled and the stigma has receded a bit into the false pod, the bud is ready to pick.

At the point of maturity, the cola fluoresces. This is caused by light refracting from the tiny glands filled with THC. The bud looks like a jewel-encrusted flower.

The number of days from onset of flowering to maturity varies depending on variety and the length of the dark period. The shorter the dark period, the faster the flowers mature. However, when the flowers are brought to maturity faster, they are smaller than when they are given more time to mature. For instance, a bud under a regimen of 12 hours of darkness may take eight weeks to mature. The same bud, kept under a 14-hour darkness regimen, may take only six weeks to mature, but may weigh 25% less than the longer maturing bud.

The flowering cycle may be started at 12 hours of darkness. After four to six weeks, the dark part of the cycle may be increased to 14 to 16 hours of darkness and the buds will mature quickly.

Sometimes parts of the bud mature, but the bud continues to produce new growth. Buds should be picked when the rate of this growth slows. The mature parts of the bud can be removed using a small pair of scissors. Some varieties respond to pruning by continuing to produce new growth.

The top buds may mature while buds lower in the plant or lower on the branch are still immature. The mature buds should be cut. This opens the lower buds to direct light and promotes ripening in ten to fifteen days. The under-canopy usually occurs when the lower branches aren't cut in the vegetative and early flowering stages. A good part of the plant's energy, and thus yield, is invested in the lower secondary flowers.

A few varieties, including Thai and other Southeast Asian plants, are natural hermaphrodites, which produce flowers intermittently under a 12-hour regimen. They have adapted to the latitude in Thailand, which is close to the equator and does not have much seasonal variation of daylight hours. Colombian varieties have also adapted to low latitude conditions by prolonging flowering a bit, until it catches up with a chronological schedule. These varieties are not recommended for indoor growth since they take months to mature fully.

Some indica varieties produce male flowers just as they mature. This is not a problem. It can be considered a sign of ripening and an indication that the buds are ready for picking.

CHAPTER 17

HARVEST

The buds are ready when the stigma has dried and turned color, and the ovary behind the stigma has swelled as if it was pollinated. The glands, which cover the surface of the leaves, the false seed pod and most of the growth surrounding them, have swelled to fluorescence.

No bud should be cut before its time. Depending on the variety and the density of the canopy either the top buds or the side buds may finish first. If the canopy is loose so that light penetrates to lower portions of the plant, it is likely that some of the lower buds may finish first. If the canopy is tight, then the top buds will finish first.

If the lower canopy is left on the plants for another seven to fifteen days after the top part is picked, it will ripen. Some varieties develop new growth with this treatment, others just ripen. If the plants were well pruned and each has only a few leads, it is likely that all of the buds on the plant will be finished at the same time.

If a uniform garden is being grown, containing clones of one variety, all the plants will ripen at the same time. If the garden is composed of several varieties, the top buds of the garden will probably ripen over a two week period. Once again, the under-canopy will not be ripe.

Once the buds ripen, it is time to cut. The entire plant may be cut, even unripe under-canopy, so that new plants can be placed in the garden, or only the buds may be cut as they ripen, leaving the under-canopy to ripen. This is usually done in multi-variety gardens. Since it

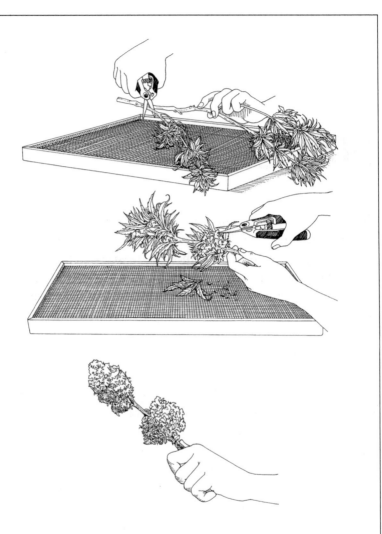

Manicuring a Bud

This plant is being manicured over a 100 strand per inch mesh screen to catch fallen glands. They drop through it to be collected later. The stems are first cut from the branch and then the larger leaves are cut from the stems. Finally the smaller leaves are trimmed off of the buds.

will take more time for the top bud of some varieties to ripen, the under-canopy of earlier harvested plants may as well be left to ripen.

If possible, before the marijuana is dried, it should be manicured. All the large leaves are removed, leaving only buds and the small leaves surrounding them. All of these parts are totally covered with glands filled with cannabinoids.

The leaves which were clipped off can be used in cooking or rubbed against a 100-line mesh screen or silk scarf to remove the glands. These glands are loose hash. If they are heated a little and pressed together, they congeal and form a hard piece just like imported hashish.

A few buds can be easily dried by placing them in a loosely folded brown paper bag at room temperature. Larger amounts are hung or placed on trays in a dark area, such as a closet.

The buds smoke best if they are cured before they are dried. This is done by providing a steady stream of fairly moist 70°F air for two to three days. This gives the plant material time to continue metabolizing, turning some of the starches back to sugars, creating a smoother taste. Then the temperature is raised to 85°F and the humidity lowered. The circulating air quickly dries the bud.

Buds can be dried quickly, too with hot, dry air. If the bud is high quality, there will be only subtle differences in taste between the two methods. This may be the only real possibility if the space or inclination to go through a more elaborate process is not available.

The plants have been harvested. They are drying. How long must a grower wait before tasting some? Just a few minutes! While this is not the best way of drying, because the taste is slightly harsher with less aroma, the microwave can be used to dry the bud, leaving the potency intact. The wet bud should be placed in the microwave for 30-second periods until it is sufficiently dry.

Oven drying is riskier. If the temperature is too warm, the THC evaporates and is totally lost, so the oven is kept at a low temperature, about 100°F.

The buds are considered dry when they have lost most of their water but still have a little pliability. They should burn well at this point. When the buds are drier, they retain their potency but lose some of the aroma and they burn more harshly.

Once the buds are dry, they should be stored. THC, the main active ingredient in marijuana, is destroyed by light and heat in the presence of oxygen. The best way to store it would be in a jar filled with carbon dioxide, nitrogen or another inert gas which is placed in a refrigerator or, for longer storage, in the freezer. Stored in a cool environment like that, the marijuana will stay fresh for years.

Most people do not store their bud in exotic gases. However, it is advisable to store most of the stash in a container in the cold and dark and only keep out stash to be used within the next few days.

For long term storage, marijuana should be stored in hard plastic, glass, metal or wood containers. When closed, these containers should seal tightly.

For convenience, most commercial marijuana is sold in Zip-Loc™ bags. These bags carry an electrical charge which attracts the glands. The inner surfaces of used bags are frequently covered with glands. For this reason these bags should not be used to hold marijuana, especially for long periods of time.

CHAPTER 18

RESTARTING

Restarting the marijuana garden is easy.

First, all water should be drained from the system and the reservoirs washed with an ammonia solution. The trays and containers should be washed or soaked and rinsed.

Compared to its yield, the cost of filling the indoor garden with medium, even expensive mediums, is very low. Rather than reusing the medium, it is easier and safer to throw it away, use it in a different type of garden, or contribute it to a community garden program, than to take the chance of spreading an infection to the new plants.

However, if there were no infections in the garden, it can be reused. First, it is removed from the containers and the roots and stems removed from the medium as much as possible. Any clumps are broken up, so it flows freely. Modifications such as compost, humus or worm castings should be added if you wish to use nutritive supplements. If the medium has broken down a bit and become finer, perlite, pebbles or bark should be added to prevent packing and insure good drainage.

Pebbles, gravel or hydro-stones should be thoroughly washed and rinsed.

Rockwool slabs and cubes can be reused too, although few growers do it. As long as it retains its shape, it is suitable for the garden. Roots should be removed as much as possible by pulling or cutting them. This is easier to do when the cubes or slabs have dried out a little.

When working with any of these materials, it is best as always to have a well ventilated space, use a face mask and be fully clothed.

The walls should be washed down and the reflective material cleaned. Floors should be vacuumed and washed if appropriate. The lamps or fluorescent tubes should be unplugged and cleaned so the light can get through. The reflector should also be cleaned.

Almost every gardener makes improvements as the room evolves. Repairs or modifications should also be made now.

After the garden has been cleaned, the planting material replaced or renewed, and any repairs or changes made, it is time to replant.

Whether seeds or clones are being used, they should have been started a month previously. At this time, they should be six to ten inches tall and should have four or five sets of leaves. Each set is larger than the previous one and the number of fingers has increased. They should be placed in the garden as described in Chapter 16.

CHAPTER 19

PROBLEMS

Every gardener faces some problems with the garden at one time or another. Environmental problems, insects, and diseases can create havoc among the plants, and often leave the grower stumped.

The best way gardeners have prevented problems has been to carefully examine the garden at least once a week. First, a gardener looks at the entire space. Do the plants look healthy and vigorous? Is their color normal and bright? Then, the grower examines a few plants close up. Do they look healthy? Have they grown since the last examination? Do the leaves or any other plant parts show signs of nutrient problems? Taking a photographer's 4X or 8X loupe, available at camera stores, the cultivator looks at the leaves of several plants and asks, "Are there any abnormalities? Any insects or eggs on the undersides?"

The most common problems with plants are not pests. They are overwatering, underwatering, and over-fertilization.

WATERING PROBLEMS

When the medium is waterlogged, the roots cannot obtain enough oxygen. At the same time, anaerobic bacteria, which are active in oxygen-free environments, attack the roots and produce ammonia, which has a distinctive odor. Plant leaves curl and the leaves turn unhealthy dark green from lack of oxygen. Waterlogged medium is not usually a problem for hydroponic gardeners, but may occur in some planting mixes. The solution is to let the medium dry out a bit and to water the plant less.

Roots have a harder time drawing water as the medium dries. During the light hours, the need for water is especially acute. If the roots have no moisture, first the bottom leaves and then the entire plant start to wilt. Water must be added before the leaves die, which can be only a matter of hours. The old myth that water-stressing the plant increases potency is not relevant to indoor cultivation.

FERTILIZING PROBLEMS

Slight chronic over-fertilizing can cause the leaves to curl either upward or underneath. Heavy over-fertilizing can cause the plant to wilt in a matter of minutes, because the medium has a higher concentration of salts (nutrients) than the plant and will thus draw water from the plant.

Once the plant starts to wilt from over-fertilizing a few minutes may mean life or death. The solution to this problem is to get rid of the excess nutrient by rinsing it out of the medium. If the plant recovers it will take several days. Some of the large leaves may die. Within seven to ten days the plant should resume vigorous growth.

pH

Marijuana sometimes suffers from improper pH. When the water and medium is kept in a pH range of 6.2–6.8, the nutrients will be readily soluble and available to the plants. When the pH moves out of the 6.2–6.8 range, nutrients precipitate out of solution and become unavailable to the plant. In both soil and hydroponic systems the best way to solve this problem is by adjusting the water-nutrient solution with either pH Up or Down, as discussed earlier in Chapter 14.

The nutrient deficiencies that a plant is most likely to encounter are iron (Fe), magnesium (Mg) nitrogen (N), phosphorous (P), potassium (K) and zinc (Zn). the symptoms and cures of each of these deficiencies are listed in Chapter 14.

PESTS

The best way to deal with pests is to prevent them from infecting the garden. No one should go to the indoor garden after being in the yard or around outdoor plants. Pests might be inadvertently carried in. While they are kept in check naturally outdoors, they have a field day indoors where there is a much less hostile environment. Healthy plants should be kept away from infected plants and should not be handled after handling infected ones. The pests most likely to infect an indoor garden are mites, white flies, aphids and thrips.

MITES

Mites are not insects but arachnids, related to spiders. They are very small and look like tiny brown, red, or black dots on the undersides of leaves. The first indication of their presence is usually a brown spot of dead tissue (necrosis) which can be seen on the top of the leaf where they have been sucking. The infection may not be noticed until after there are between ten and fifty suckers on a leaf. Using a magnifier, a grower will notice them walking around on their eight legs when they are not sucking the plant dry.

Mites breed very quickly, going from egg to sexually mature adult in about 14 days. They like large families and they are very difficult to control. They thrive in a dry environment. High humidity and low temperatures slow them down. They are very difficult to eliminate.

If only a few plants are lightly infected, carefully removing them from the garden may be the best idea. The plant should be cut at ground level, placed in a plastic bag, and removed from the garden.

There are several sprays and dips which may eliminate mites. Pyrethrum may work, but sometimes mites are resistant to this natural organic pesticide. Before budding, a soap dip with pyrethrum and nicotine sulfate (or some cigarette tobacco) will knock down the population. However, the mite eggs may be unaffected, so the plants should be dipped every three days for two weeks.

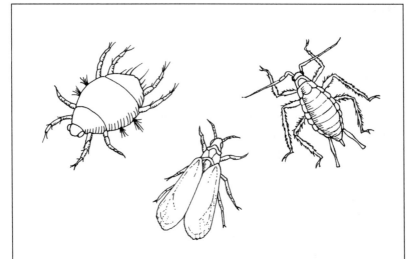

Mite

These $1/32$" relatives of spiders are a garden's most dangerous pest. They suck plant juices and multiply quickly until they overwhelm the plant. Treatments: Pyrethrum, Malathion, other botanicals, Predatory Mites and other predators.

Aphid

Adult aphids are about $1/16$" long and come in many colors. Easily eliminated if dealt with promptly; devastating if not. Treatments: Pyrethrum, various predators.

Whitefly

These $1/8$" long plant suckers are vectors for disease. They are easily spotted flying around weakened plants and should be eliminated at first sight. Treatments: Pyrethrum, Encarseria Formosa and other predators.

Malathion is a pesticide registered for vegetables and may be needed to eliminate the pests. It can be used as a spray, but breathing it should be avoided. so it may be more practical to use it as a dip. It is usually effective against mites, but not their eggs. Some mites have developed resistance to it, too.

Summer oil can be sprayed on vegetative plants or used in dips. It forms a thin film which does minimal damage to the plant tissue, but smothers the mites. It is moderately effective, and enhances other sprays.

Hydrogen peroxide is also used as a pesticide ingredient at the rate of one-and-one-half ounces 3.5% H_2O_2 per pint of water. It can be used as a spray or dip. One grower recommends a spray of eight ounces each distilled water and sugar. Boil until the sugar is dissolved. Add one-and-one-half ounces 3.5% H_2O_2. He claims that when the plants are dipped or sprayed, the liquid kills mites on contact. Instead of sugar, I would use water with a wetting agent, which would help it to spread evenly.

There are quite a few pesticides in the garden shop which list mites as targets on their labels. Unfortunately, most of these are registered only for ornamentals, which means that they should not be used on food crops. I would not use a pesticide that is not registered for food on marijuana.

Once established, predator mites, which feed on their genetic cousins, keep the pest population under control. According to instruction sheets it may take several introductions to get them started. There are several different species of predator mites, each of which does best at a slightly different temperature range. Usually mixed species are introduced to hobby gardens. Although some growers swear by them, I have never seen them actually control a mite infestation.

Spider mite destroyers are tiny ladybugs $1/25''$ long. They eat up to 40 mites per day each. They are sold in batches of 100 and develop a self-sustaining colony.

Ladybugs in indoor gardens do eat mites but they have a fatal attraction to the lamps, which they fly into, resulting in their immediate incineration. Ladybug users report success keeping them alive by spraying them with Coca Cola® which glues their wings so they can't fly. Instead, they walk through the garden, eating mites.

APHIDS

Aphids are oval insects about $^1/_{16}$" long that come in a rainbow of colors including white, green, red-brown, and black. They are soft-skinned and are often farmed by ants, which squeeze them for their "honeydew," which is a sugar concentrate. Aphids, looking for protein, suck on plants. The excess sugars are exuded onto plants and these areas become hot spots for fungal and other infections. Aphids breed very quickly, and like warm, dry climates.

If there are aphids around, look for ant colonies. These should be eliminated using ant bait or traps.

There are several insects which may be able to control aphids in the garden. The predatory gall midge feasts on aphids in its larval stage and can adapt to greenhouse conditions. Aphids are also a favorite food of ladybugs.

Aphids are usually susceptible to soapy water-pyrethrum sprays. A much more effective dip has recently become available. Aphids can also be virtually eliminated using Botanigard.™ This spray contains a fungus which attacks aphids, whiteflies and thrips. It is probably the easiest and safest spray to use. It is harmless to humans and pets and is registered for use on food crops up to day of harvest.

WHITEFLIES

Whiteflies look just like houseflies except when they are only about $^1/_{10}$" to $^1/_5$" long, and are all white. They also suck plant juices and multiply quickly. They fly around the plants when they are disturbed.

Encarseria formosa are about one-quarter the size of whiteflies and are harmless to humans and pests, but not to whiteflies. They are very tiny wasps which do not bite or sting, and are nonsocial: they do not have nests. They parasitize the whitefly eggs, laying their eggs inside them. Once released, they fly around and live in the garden, but are rarely seen.

Whitefly predators are a tiny black ladybug species with a voracious appetite for whitefly eggs and larvae. They adapt to indoor conditions and are used in conjunction with the wasps for more complete control.

Until wasps are introduced, the aphid population is kept in check using pyrethum sprays. The wasps are susceptible to sprays, so growers do not spray for several days before a release.

Botanigard™ spray, mentioned above, virtually eliminates whiteflies from the grow space within a few weeks.

THRIPS

Thrips are tiny insects $1/32$"–$1/16$" long. They live on top of the leaf and leave a trail as they eat the top tissue.

They can be eliminated using a combination of minute pirate bugs (orius insidiosis) and soil nematodes. The orius is about $1/20$" long and uses its beak to pierce holes in thrips and suck its' victims dry. If thrip populations are large, the orius will kill more than it sucks.

Thrip predator mites are very tiny and feed on thrips and pollen. They can be used in conjunction with pirate bugs to control thrip populations.

Soil nematodes are predators which eat insects that are in the soil. They are effective in helping to stop thrip infections.

Soap, pyrethrum, summer oil and nicotine sprays or dip also knock them out of the garden as does Botanigard.™

Also Available at Your Local Bookstore

Marijuana Question? ASK ED
by Ed Rosenthal

The Encyclopedia of Marijuana, this book contains everything you ever wanted to know, from cultivation to inhaling. Compiled from the popular *High Times* column, the questions have been rearranged by subject for easy reference and the responses have been revised, clarified and expanded.

Most growers will find themselves referring to this book more than to any other cultivation manual. With its comprehensive table of contents and index, it's the trouble shooters companion. **$19.95**

CO₂, Temperature & Humidity
by D. Gold, edited by Ed Rosenthal

Double your yield! Carbon Dioxide can increase a garden's yield by up to 100%. This book shows how to use CO_2 simply, effectively, and easily. Safe techniques are given for enriching the garden with this important nutrient. **$12.95**

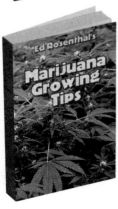

Marijuana Growing Tips
by Ed Rosenthal

A "must read" for cannabis lovers. This book offers Ed's best growing tips. Everything from selecting seeds, to artificial lighting to hydroponics. Contains a revealing in-depth talk with Carlton Turner, former director of the U.S. government farm. **$12.95**

Also Available at Your Local Bookstore

Marijuana Grower's Handbook

Expert Ed Rosenthal takes you through the entire life cycle of the marijuana plant, giving advice from seed selection to harvesting.

Ed explains the factors that influence:
- Growth rate
- Light
- CO_2
- Temperature
- Nutrients
- Water

A great index, bibliography, tables, and charts make this one of the easiest reference books available for marijuana enthusiasts. A new chapter provides tips and solutions to the most common indoor growing problems. With a color section that includes photos from the top Seed Companies and the newest grow systems.

"Ed, the famous Ask Ed... is an entire set of encyclopedias when it comes to growing pot. If knowledge is power, Ed Rosenthal is General Electric."
— Dr. A. Sumach, *Cannabis Culture*

"He's the man who wrote the book on growing pot; a world travelled cannabis researcher who's brought back cultivation secrets from every part of the globe."
— *High Times*

$19.95

Also Available at Your Local Bookstore

Marihuana Reconsidered
by Dr. Lester Grinspoon, M.D.

Back in print! First published by Harvard University press in 1971, this is still the most comprehensive assessment of marihuana and its place in society. Noted psychiatrist, Dr. Lester Grinspoon pulverizes the arguments that keep marihuana illegal. Updated with a new introduction by the author, who still believes that the most dangerous thing about smoking marihuana is getting caught.   **$19.95**

Why Marijuana Should Be Legal
by Ed Rosenthal and Steve Kubby

This concise and pointed argument should be on every smoker's bookshelf. Logical, no-nonsense discussions of the costs, benefits, and implication of the legalization of marijuana will help you convince anyone that legalizing pot is the right way to go.   **$9.95**

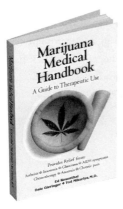

Marijuana Medical Handbook
by Ed Rosenthal, Dale Gieringer, and Tod Mikuriya, M.D.

This guide offers information on how to use and procure marijuana for medicine. It provides the most up-to-date, scientific methods for processing your marijuana. A concise cultivation section by expert Ed Rosenthal explains plant basics and shows an easy way to set up a personal use garden.   **$16.95**

Also Available at Your Local Bookstore

The Joint Rolling Handbook

Easy-to-follow instructions and stunning graphics show high-rollers how to set up and assemble the finest smoking tools. With a spaced out rabbit as your spiritual guide, master the art of joint rolling. Everything you ever needed to know: from the most basic Saturday Night Special, the mind boggling complexity of the Crossroads, and the legendary Cannabis Cigar.

$9.95

Stir Crazy: Cooking with Cannabis

Stir Crazy's easy-to-follow instructions and stunning graphics show would-be marijuana connoisseurs how to prepare the finest meals with an added dash of taste. With a wacky rabbit as your culinary guide, master the art of entertaining and learn why marijuana is the most essential ingredient in the gourmet's kitchen. Everything you ever needed to know: from the most basic cooking techniques to the mind-boggling complexity of washing up. And for the concerned or curious, health information, legal tips and a history of marijuana use are also included.

$9.95

Also Available at Your Local Bookstore

Ecstasy: Dance, Trance & Transformation

• What is Ecstasy?

• Is E an aphrodisiac?

• Is Ecstasy addictive?

• Does Ecstasy harm brain cells?

• How dangerous is Ecstasy?

• How can you tell what is in a pill?

• Does herbal Ecstasy work and is it safe?

Ecstasy: Dance, Trance & Transformation is the most comprehensive source of information about Ecstasy and the dance culture. This book looks at Ecstasy in the US — laws, music, and users — and the global scene. A valuable book for anyone who uses Ecstasy or has ever thought of taking it.

$19.95

Psilocybin
by O.T. Oss and O.N. Oeric
Foreword by Terrence McKenna

The revised and expanded edition of the classic how-to manual of psilocybin mushroom cultivation. In-depth growing instructions with step-by-step photographs showing exactly how it is done. The rediscovery of the mushroom and its historical use in ritual is also covered.

$16.95

ONLINE AT WWW.QUICKTRADING.COM

www.quicktrading.com

online home of Ask Ed™

Grow Tips

Politics

Links to the best cannabis sites

Buds

Marijuana Question:
Come online and Ask Ed